——— THE ART OF THE ———
WORLD'S GREATEST
WATERCOLOURISTS

THE ART OF THE
WORLD'S GREATEST
WATERCOLOURISTS

FIONA AND ISLA HACKNEY

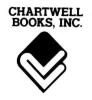

CHARTWELL BOOKS, INC.

A QUINTET BOOK

Published by Chartwell Books
A Division of Book Sales, Inc.
110 Enterprise Avenue
Secaucus, New Jersey 07094

ISBN 1-55521-568-8

This book was designed and produced by
Quintet Publishing Limited
6 Blundell Street
London N7 9BH

Creative Director: Peter Bridgewater
Art Director: Ian Hunt
Designer: Sally McKay
Project Editor: Caroline Beattie
Contributing Editor: Angie Gair
Picture Researcher: Liz Eddison

Typeset in Great Britain by
Central Southern Typesetters, Eastbourne
Manufactured in Hong Kong by
Regent Publishing Services Limited
Printed in Hong Kong by
Leefung-Asco Printers Limited

CONTENTS

CHAPTER ONE

ORIGINS AND ANTECEDENTS

Splashed-ink landscape by Sesshu, given by the
artist to his pupil. He went to China to learn this
particular technique. The influence of China
upon Japanese art is widespread.

*I*t was not until the 18th century that watercolour paintings truly became accepted as works of art in their own right; yet water-based paint dates from the earliest days of human history. Some 40,000 years ago, primitive humans began to make pigments extracted from animal, mineral and plant sources, dried and ground to a powder and bound with gum or animal fat, then diluted with water. Artists used these colours to create vivid and lifelike pictures of animals on the walls of caves. For reasons unknown, these paintings were hidden in remote, dark caverns deep underground, and have survived undisturbed until relatively recent times. The first discovery of cave paintings was made in the late 19th century at Altamira in Spain, and another major discovery was made at Lascaux in France in 1940. It is widely accepted that these prehistoric paintings are of a remarkably high artistic standard.

In Ancient Egypt, painted reliefs were used to decorate the walls of palaces and tombs. Artists worked with pigments derived mainly from minerals such as iron oxide (red), silica (blue), malachite (green), carbon (black) and gypsum (white), and these were ground in water and bound with gum, starch or honey. Due to the mineral content of the paints, the colours produced were quite intense, and have retained their vividness over the centuries.

Ancient forms of watercolour were opaque, not transparent, and applied thickly to the rough, non-absorbent surfaces of caves and buildings. Early forms of paper (made from papyrus reeds) and parchment (made from animal skins) also lacked the brilliance and absorbency to allow watercolours to be rendered transparently; the richly decorated religious scripts of the early centuries AD, for example, were painted opaquely and often overlaid with gold leaf. Indeed, it was not until the 18th century that the distinction between body colour and transparent watercolour became a subject for heated debate.

Watercolour painting in China evolved in a different direction to that of western Europe. Chinese artists used soft-haired brushes and worked on silk and rice paper, whose absorbent surfaces encouraged the use of delicate, transparent washes and softly gradated forms. Chinese painting embodied a poetic contemplation of nature; with just a few delicate strokes, artists captured a mood of mystery and atmospheric space in their landscapes, anticipating by several centuries the work of western watercolour masters such as Turner and Girtin.

DÜRER: THE FATHER OF WATERCOLOUR

The first European to use watercolour extensively, and to capitalize on its transparent qualities, was the German Renaissance artist Albrecht Dürer (1471–1528). Dürer trained as a painter and engraver, and his sensitive awareness of line is reflected in the hundreds of meticulous studies of animals, plants and flowers which he produced for his own use and pleasure. Dürer was no purist when it came to handling the watercolour medium: he used transparent washes to capture the play of light, opaque colour to sculpt the forms, and touches of pen and ink to accentuate linear details.

In 1490 Dürer journeyed across the Alps to Italy, where he saw the work of his Renaissance contemporaries and was impressed by it. At this time he also began to paint landscapes in watercolour. Unique among his contemporaries, he exploited the transparency and delicacy of watercolour: building up thin layers of colour and allowing brushstrokes to merge while still wet, he captured the subtle nuances of atmosphere and colour in the landscape, caused by the effects of aerial perspective. The free, sketch-like quality of paintings such as *Pond in the Woods* and *Italian Mountains* anticipates the approach adopted by Cézanne some 400 years later. Dürer is thus the artist who, more than any other, deserves to be considered the 'father' of modern watercolour.

Increasingly, Dürer became interested in colour for its own sake, and explored its unique ability to convey an impression of shifting light. A passage from his notes on painting provides an insight into his method and technique:

Be careful that thou shade each colour with a similar colour. Thus I hold that a yellow, to retain its kind, must be shaded with a yellow, darker toned than the principal colour. If thou shade it with green or blue, it remaineth no longer in keeping but becometh thereby a shot colour, like the colour of silk shifts woven of threads of two colours ... Happen what may, every colour must in shading keep its class.

....
R I G H T **The Great Piece of Turf** – *Albrecht Dürer, 1507. In their obsessive attention to botanical details, Dürer's watercolours of plantforms represent an important tradition in the use of watercolour for pseudo-scientific purposes.*
....

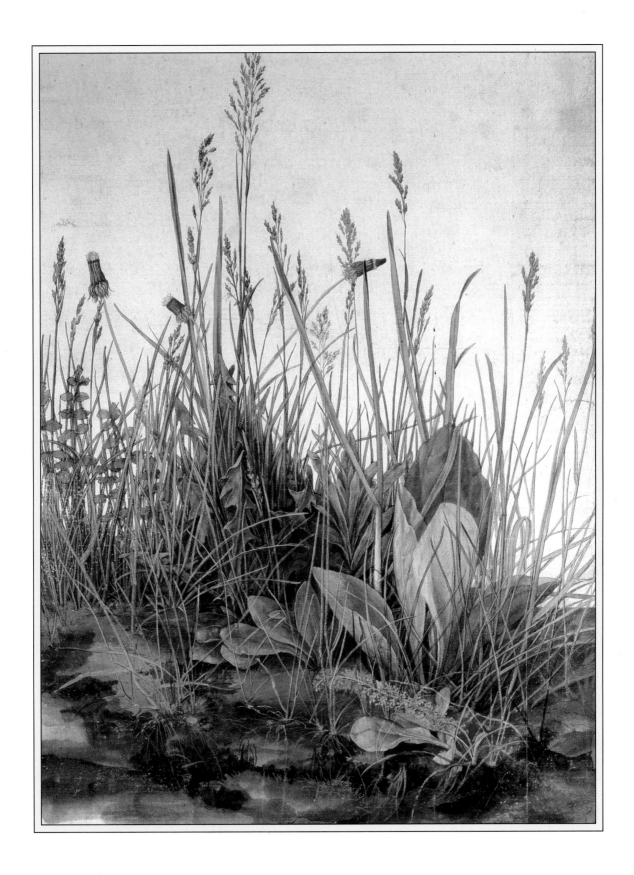

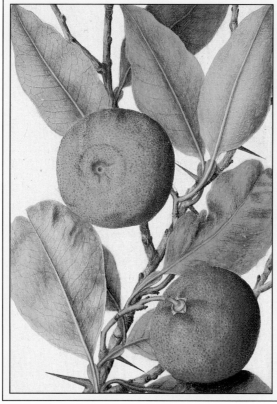

R I G H T Orange Blossom
– *Jacques le Moyne De
Morgues. An engraved book
produced from these
watercolours of fruit and
flowers by Jacques le Moyne
de Morgues was dedicated to
the wife of Sir Philip Sidney.
The microscopic exactness of
this illustration demonstrates
the artist's skill as a
draughtsman and colourist.*

R I G H T Cottage with
Outhouse and
Agricultural Implements –
*Adrian van Ostade. Here the
emphasis is on outline: the
drawing is completed without
the addition of colour, which
was used chiefly to give
additional substance to
individual objects.*

The history of watercolour painting does not follow a smooth and steady path; not only did Dürer's art stand apart from the mainstream of its day, it remained isolated for nearly 300 years. Inexplicably, Dürer himself abandoned the watercolour medium and turned to other areas. Despite the acclaim which his pictures received, watercolour fell back into obscurity after his death – regarded as a secondary medium suitable for preparatory studies for architectural and ornamental designs, tapestries, and of course oil paintings.

BOTANICAL ART

One area in which watercolour did come into its own was in the field of botany and natural history. The Renaissance – which spanned the 15th and 16th centuries – saw a reawakening of interest in the sciences, and illustrators and illuminators recorded, in minute detail, their native flora and fauna using watercolour and body colour.

From the 16th century, many European countries were engaged in great voyages of discovery and exploration and set up colonies in the New World. Illustrators and botanists accompanying the explorers produced paintings of exotic flora and fauna, which were often the only means of bringing their discoveries home. Watercolour, with its speed and simplicity, was found to be the ideal medium for the purpose, as it allowed colours and tones to be built up gradually to precise requirements and the smallest details could be rendered with the tip of the brush. One of the best known botanical artists of the time was John White, who went to Florida in 1564 and also sailed with Sir Walter Raleigh's 1585 expedition to North America. White made full and effective use of the watercolour medium in his records of the scenery of the North Carolina coast, and of the way of life of the Eskimo and Indian population. On his return to England in 1586, his pictures reached a wide literate public through the engravings of Theodore de Bry, published in his great work *America*.

De Bry also published the work of Jacques Le Moyne de Morgues, who, exiled from France for his Huguenot sympathies, settled in London in 1581 and produced beautiful botanical illustrations of the flowers and fruits then most common in English gardens.

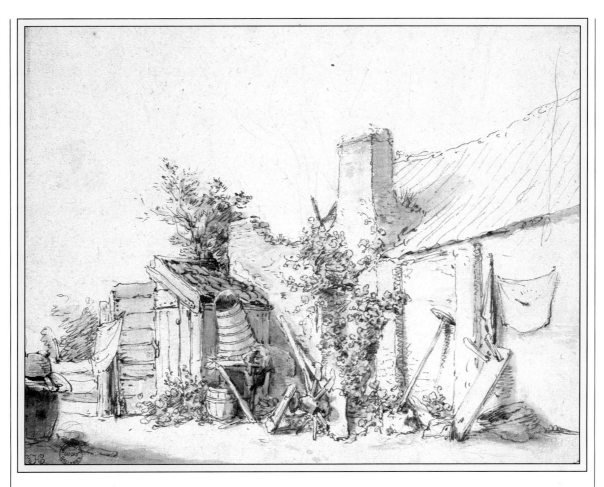

THE DUTCH SCHOOL

Because watercolour took root and flourished so strongly in Britain after the late 18th century, it is often assumed that the medium was a British invention – a belief much encouraged by English commentators of the time. In the Somerset Gazette of 1823, WH Pyne comments:

> With reference to Water Colour Painting, we have to speak of a new art, originating with the English, and perfected with the age whence it began . . . It is something to record that the invention of painting in water colours, certainly one of the most elegant and interesting studies that has emanated from human ingenuity, is of English birth, of English growth, and on our soil has arrived to maturity.

Despite these claims, watercolour was in reality a foreign import, coming originally from Continent Europe, and in particular from the Netherlands, particularly influential in this regard.

During the latter half of the 16th century, flower growing was a national passion in the Netherlands, and wealthy gardeners often commissioned paintings of flowers, fruits and butterflies. Watercolour, with its delicacy and transparency, enabled artists to record their subjects with an almost scientific precision, and the paintings of artists such as Ambrosius Bosschaert, Jacob de Gheyn and the Flemish Georg Hoefnagel were in great demand.

By the 17th century, watercolours in the Netherlands were becoming increasingly accepted as finished works in their own right, and not merely as preliminary studies for oil paintings. This was an era of economic prosperity, and the paintings of the time reflect the preoccupations of an independent, largely Protestant, mercantile people. Hendrik Avercamp's open-air scenes of skaters on frozen canals and van Ostade's rustic interiors display a delight in the world of ordinary people who were recorded doing everyday activities in everyday situations.

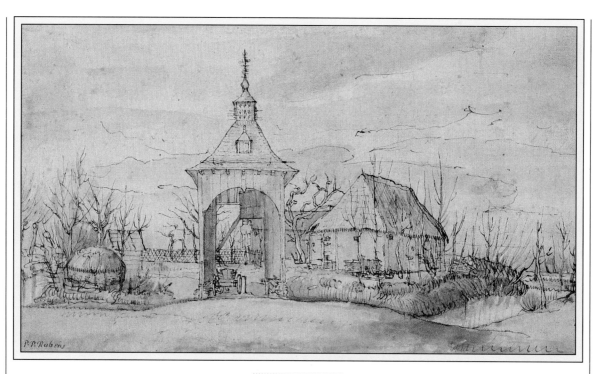

....
A B O V E A Moated Grange with a Bridge
House – *Peter Paul Rubens. Landscape
painting was brought to London when Rubens
came to the Court of Charles I in 1629.*
....

The Dutch and Flemish also played an important part in the development of landscape painting – an art form still alien in England at the beginning of the 17th century. Around 1600, landscape painting is described by one English writer as:

> an art so new in England, and so lately come a shore, as all the language within our four seas cannot find it a Name, but a borrowed one (*Landscape* is the Dutch *Landschap*) and that from a people that are no great lenders but upon good securities, the Dutch. Perhaps they will name their owne Child. For to say truth the Art is theirs!

Initially the emphasis in Dutch landscapes was on accurate topographical renderings, encouraged by collectors who commissioned views, called 'atlases', of their native towns and villages. Later, artists began to paint naturalistic landscapes and genre scenes for their own pleasure, often working from direct observation, in the open air. In the 1640s Allart van Everdigen painted romantic watercolours depicting mountain scenes in Sweden – an approach which evolved into the 19th century English taste for the Sublime.

ANTHONY VAN DYCK

In the rest of Europe, meanwhile, there were no major painters using watercolour as an end in itself. Then, more than a century after Dürer's death, watercolour at last took an important step forward with the work of Anthony van Dyck (1599–1641). A former pupil of Rubens, van Dyck settled in London in 1632 and became court painter to Charles I. Although best known as a portraitist, van Dyck also made landscape sketches in watercolour. These were only a small part of his tremendous output as a painter, yet they were to have an important influence on the future development of English landscape painting. Van Dyck's watercolours broke new ground in their freedom of brushwork and deliberately sketchy, unfinished effect. Works such as *A Country Lane* are rendered with fluid and transparent washes and convey a real sense of the natural scene with its shifting pools of light and shadow. The result of van Dyck's *plein-airist* technique is an effect of freshness and movement which anticipates 19th century masters such as Girtin and Constable.

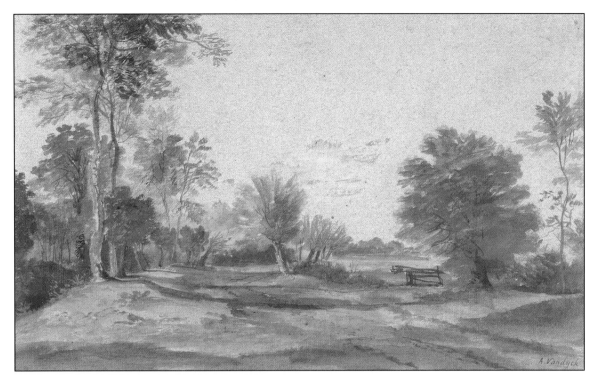

....
ABOVE **A Country Lane** – *Anthony Van Dyck. Van Dyck's works depend for their effect on colour rather than line: 'local colour' is painted and shadow is indicated by the addition of a darker colour. The resulting impression of light and atmosphere anticipates the 19th-century work of John Constable.*
....

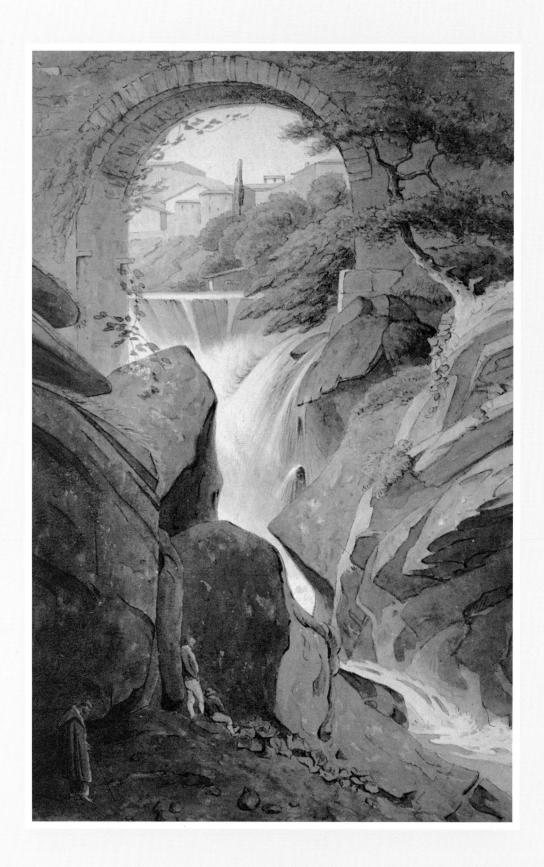

CHAPTER TWO

THE 18th CENTURY

The Falls of Tivoli with Three
Figures in the Foreground – *John Warwick
Smith (circle of). The drama of Italian landscape
and Alpine scenery was to fire the imaginations
of such young British artists as John Warwick
Smith, who, while travelling abroad, developed a
far broader and more adventurous style than was
his habit at home.*

The extraordinary flowering of watercolour painting in England after 1750 became, for over a century, a national phenomenon – so much so that watercolour was assumed to be a uniquely British technique. The medium steadily rose in popularity and technical achievement during the course of the century, reached dramatic heights in the final decade, and finally spread its influence to the Continent.

There were several reasons behind the meteoric rise of the English school of watercolour painting, the most important of which was probably the increasing interest in landscape painting – a subject which British painters have always had an affinity for. During the course of the century two fundamentally different kinds of landscape painting emerged: the idealized and the realistic: in other words, the Romantic and the topographic.

Topography is defined as the objective description of interesting views and places, in which the subject is carefully and realistically recorded in thin washes of colour over a monochrome underpainting. In the Romantic, or Picturesque, approach the elements of the natural scene are arranged to correspond with a particular ideal, and the emphasis is on creating the impression that a landscape makes on the spirit and the emotions.

Before moving on to a closer examination of the Romantic and topographical traditions, it might be instructive to look at some of the other reasons for the increasing acceptance of watercolour as a medium in its own right during the 18th century.

THE GRAND TOUR

Around the middle of the century, as Britain developed its trade and became prosperous, it became fashionable for the sons of wealthy families to travel to Europe (usually Holland, Germany, Austria, France and Italy) as a means of broadening their education. Many of these young tourists took painters along with them to depict scenic views of lakes, mountains and ancient monuments. Compact and convenient for travelling, watercolour was the ideal medium for recording these travels, and the paintings were later reproduced as engravings and distributed among an enthusiastic public. Thus the Grand Tour influenced artistic fashion: dramatic Alpine landscapes, classical ruins and romantic evocations of the Grand Canal dominated 18th-century painting and formed the beginnings of the Romantic movement.

MONRO'S ACADEMY

An important figure in the development of the English school was Dr Thomas Monro (1759–1833), a physician who was also a keen art collector and patron, and a gifted amateur painter. In 1793 Monro opened his own 'school' for watercolour painters, at his home in Adelphi Terrace, London, inviting young artists to come and copy drawings from his extensive collection and paying them a small fee and supper for their work. Watercolour painting owes a debt to Monro, for not only did he bring together and encourage the two greatest watercolour painters of the late 18th and early 19th centuries – Thomas Girtin and JMW Turner – he also introduced them to the masterpieces of Canaletto and the poetic landscapes of John Robert Cozens, which were to have a lasting influence on their work.

PAUL SANDBY AND THE TOPOGRAPHIC TRADITION

Topography originated with the Dutch artists: the work of Hollar and his follower Francis Place brought about an increasing interest in depicting towns and views of note in Britain, and the tradition was carried on by Paul Sandby at the beginning of his career.

It is fitting that Sandby should be regarded as the 'father of English watercolour', for it was largely due to his influence that watercolour was raised to an independent status and considered a worthy art form in its own right. Sandby began his career as a draughtsman in the drawing room at the Tower of London, making military maps and plans. After the 1745 rebellion of Bonnie Prince Charlie he was sent to Scotland to draw topographical charts for a military survey, and there he developed a love of the rugged scenery of the Highlands, which was to be depicted later in his painting.

In about 1752, Sandby settled in London and often painted in Windsor Park, where his brother Thomas, also a watercolourist, was Deputy Ranger. Despite his technical background, Sandby's work reflected an emotional response to the landscape and a delight in the effects of atmosphere and light. His Windsor Park paintings are lyrical pastoral scenes in which nature, classical architecture and figures are harmoniously integrated. He applied his colours loosely and in delicate washes to suggest the play of sunlight on foliage and the atmospheric haze of the distant horizon.

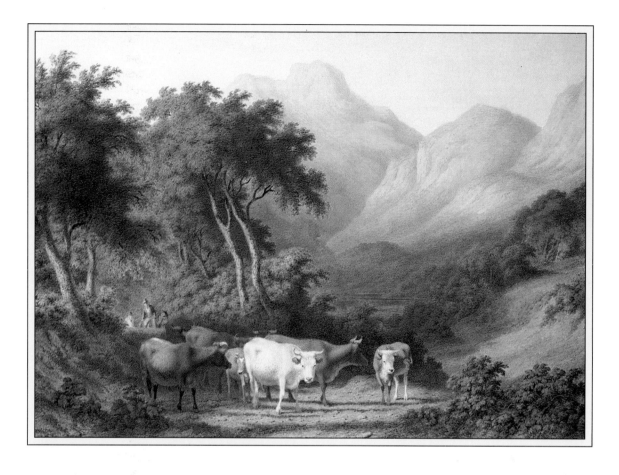

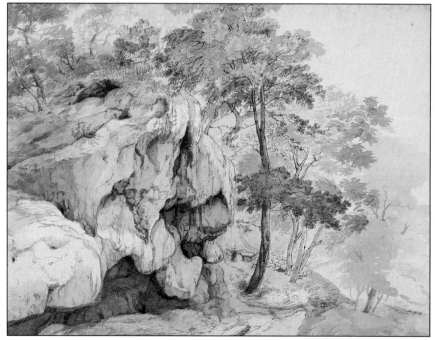

A B O V E Mountain
Scenery with Cattle –
Roberts Hills, 1839.

L E F T The Dropping
Well, Knaresborough –
*Francis Place. France Place
inherited the continental
tradition of the topographic
watercolour from Wenceslaus
Hollar, who came to England
in 1636 to work for Lord
Arundel.*

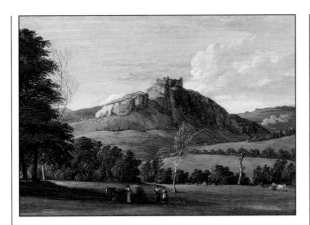

....
A B O V E Carregcennin Castle,
Carmarthenshire – *Paul Sandby. The visual
notes made on his journeys around Britain would
later be worked up into finished paintings.*
....

R I G H T Windsor Forest with Oxen
Drawing Timber – *Paul Sandby. Some 450
drawings by Paul Sandby exist at Windsor.*
....

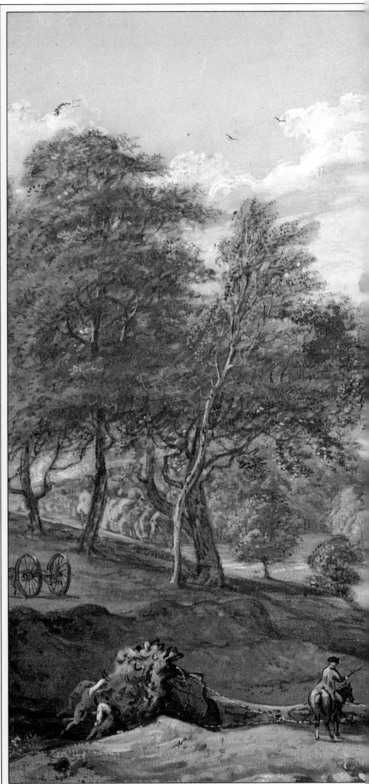

Sandby was a tireless worker. His innovative and
eclectic approach to materials was often a source of
amusement to his friends. In 1797 he wrote of:

> a grand discovery I have just made . . . a few weeks
> ago I had a French brick for breakfast; the crust
> was much burnt in the baking. I scraped off the
> black, and ground it with gum-water; it produced
> an excellent warm black colour . . .

Sandby was at the height of his career in 1768,
when he was appointed by George III as drawing-
master to the young princes. One of his other patrons,
the Hon Charles Greville, gave him the secret of
aquatint engraving, which Sandby greatly extended
as an ideal means of reproducing watercolour drawings. His subsequent published works, such as *Twelve
Views in Aquatinta from drawings taken on the spot in South
Wales* later served as a model to Turner for his *Liber
Studiorum*.

During his life Sandby worked in two recognizably
contrasting styles. The style of classical composition
which characterizes his work in body colour betrays
the influence of the Franco-Italian school, whereas
his pure watercolours were firmly rooted in the natural-
ism of the Dutch masters. This may be illustrated by
comparing Sandby's *Windsor* with his *Carrick Ferry*:
transparent watercolour was used for the former, while
the latter was executed in distemper (powdered colour

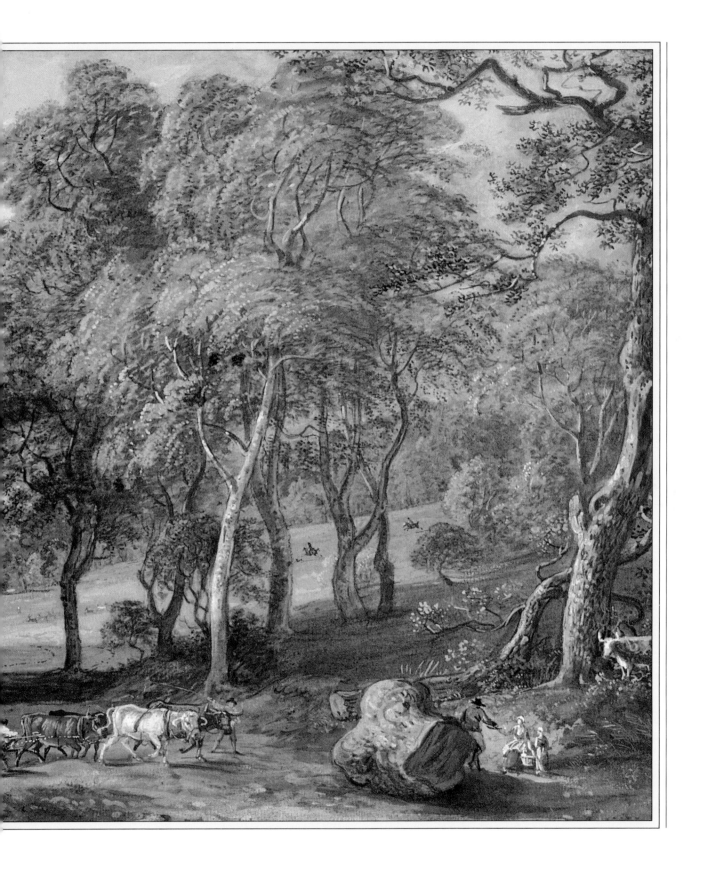

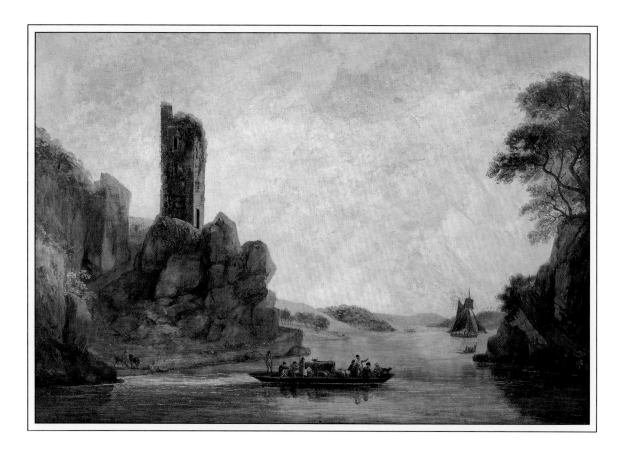

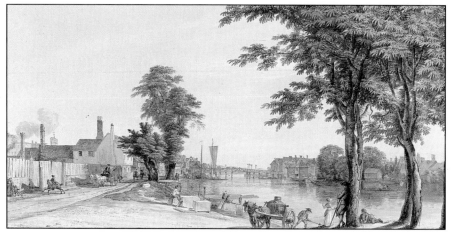

....

T O P **Carrick Ferry** – *Paul Sandby. This picture demonstrates the matt surface resultant from the use of body colour.*

....

A B O V E **Windsor, East View from Crown Corner** – *Paul Sandby. Pure watercolour produced a greater illusion of light and air.*

....

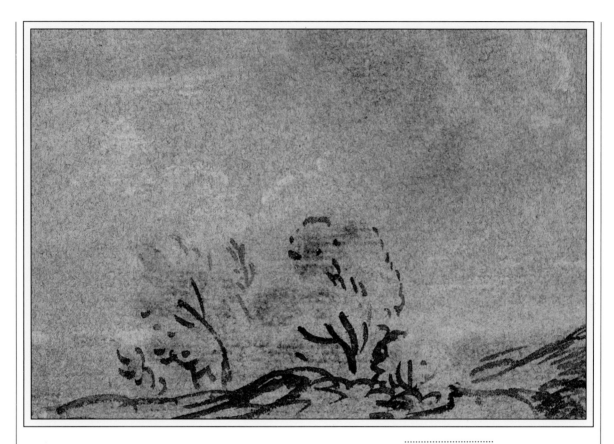

mixed with size). In *Windsor*, Sandby worked from light to dark, the whiteness of the paper lending brightness to the overlaid colours. Untouched in places, the paper shines through to provide sparkling highlights. In contrast, light effects in *Carrick Ferry* result from the addition of light tints, and the final effect is matt and opaque.

At times Sandby used a mixture of these techniques, as demonstrated by a description of Sandby's method of painting by his friend Colonel Gravatt.

> He worked his design up a good deal with transparent colours, forming a neutral tint, and then added local colours, beginning with the distance, in which his greens were formed of Naples yellow, verditer, and such-like semi-transparent colours, and in proportion, as he advanced nearer the foreground, added brown ochre, sap-green, and any strong colour that suited the purpose. The whole was laid in rather thin in the broad lights, and still more diluted in the shadows, many places left entirely without colour, which gives great air to the picture.

Sandby then went on to strengthen his composition

A B O V E Landscape Study – *Paul Sandby. Sandby experimented widely with technique; both in his role as teacher and artist he developed and codified a broad range of methods and approaches.*

with the addition of opaque lights, "plump touches" of white mixed with local colour. His extensive use of body colour established it as a recognized art form in Britain, where previously it had enjoyed little popularity. Paintings such as *Carrick Ferry*, which was exhibited at the Royal Academy in 1801, demonstrated that watercolours could be viewed alongside oils and judged their equal, as finished works of art rather than incidental drawings, sketches or designs. Sandby was greatly acclaimed in his day. Gainsborough called him "the only man of genius" who has painted "real views from Nature in this country".

Both Paul and Thomas Sandby were founder members of the Society of Artists in 1760 and of the Royal Academy in 1768, and their professional standing helped to increase the status of watercolour painting.

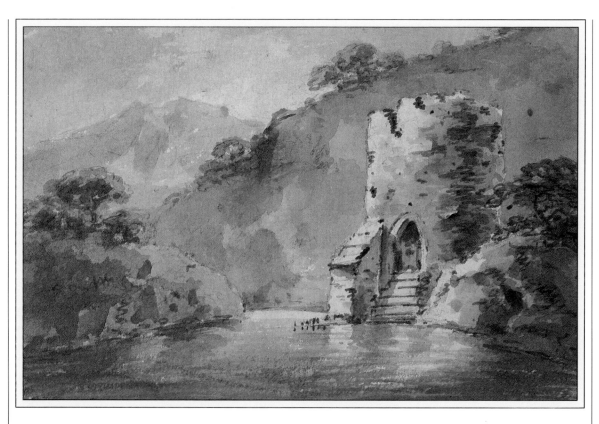

A B O V E **Ruined Tower on a River –**
*William Gilpin. In this watercolour William
Gilpin's theories of the picturesque are given
visual form, particularly in the somewhat
romantic motif of the desolate and ruined tower.*

THE EXHIBITION WATERCOLOUR

Another major factor establishing the watercolour as
a legitimate form of art was the evolution of the exhibition watercolour. Although it was not until the first
decade of the 19th century that exhibitions devoted
exclusively to the watercolour medium were promoted,
it was during the 18th century that the new art form
became officially established. Exhibiting societies such
as the Society of Artists, the Free Society and the
Royal Academy opened their galleries to artists working in watercolour from 1760s onwards. Whereas
previously the role of watercolour was directly linked
with commissions to assist engravers producing topographic records, or for clients who desired small-scale
portraits, watercolour now came to be regarded as a
suitable vehicle for artists' final statements, a medium
in which they could demonstrate their abilities, further
their ambitions and secure their future reputation.

Collectors bought them, critics reviewed them and
fellow artists, working in both watercolour and oil,
took account of and were influenced by them. Yet
even by 1791 it was still considered that truly great art
could be created only in oil or sculpture. Watercolours
were hung badly at the Academy, hidden in the smaller
room with the prints and miniatures, placed "between
windows and under windows, sometimes in the dark-
ened room with the sculpture, where if they had merit,
it could not be seen".

The immediate result of the competition with oil
painting was that watercolour artists began to experiment in order to strengthen their medium, to demonstrate that it could produce serious work of greater
size, force and strength. Watercolourists began con-
sciously to 'paint' rather than 'draw', expanding the
limits of their art both technically and expressively.
As regards technique, there were two major ones.
Bodycolour, popularized and given credibility by continental artists, was used by Academicians such as
Francesco Zuccarelli and Paul Sandby, whose works
were framed in the manner of oils. For those reluctant
to sacrifice watercolour's of transparency, drawing
became secondary to colour and tone.

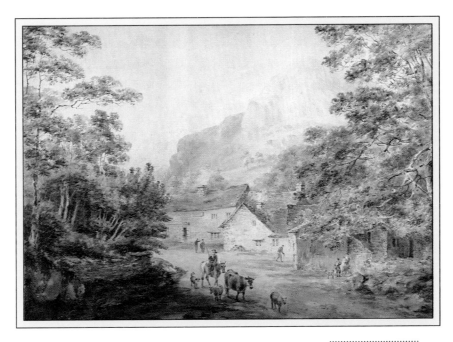

WILLIAM GILPIN AND THE
THEORISTS OF THE PICTURESQUE

A B O V E The Village of Rydal,
Westmorland – *William Sawrey Gilpin.
His brother, Rev. Gilpin, published five treatises
on the picturesque, providing a system for the
aesthetic observer and landscapist.*

As artists debated the respective merits of available techniques, the aestheticians were at work. Their ideas and theories were to give new scope to the landscapist and new significance to the art of watercolour. This section from Rev. William Gilpin's *Tour of the Lakes* conveys something of the spirit of the new approach to landscape, an approach which came to be termed the Picturesque.

> such imaginary views as give a *general idea of a country*, spread themselves more diffusely, and are carried, in the . . . imagination, through the *whole description* . . . he who works from imagination – that is, he who culls from nature the most beautiful of her productions – a *distance* here; and there a *foreground* – combines them artificially; and removing everything offensive, admits only such parts, as are *congruous*; and *beautiful*; will in all probability, make a much better landscape than he who takes it all as it comes.

Such was the popularity of these new ideas, disseminated by Gilpin's five treatises published on the subject, that the Picturesque soon acquired a cult status. Prior to Gilpin, landscape had been considered a secondary art form because it did not "improve the mind" or "excite noble sentiments". From the mid-century on, influenced by the landscapes of masters such as Claude, Poussin and Salvator Rosa and inspired by the great Italian tradition, British artists began to travel. The dramatic scenery of the Alps, Switzerland and the Mediterranean demanded a new, poetic and highly imaginative response to nature, as embodied in the work of J R Cozens, Richard Wilson, William Pars and Francis Towne.

It is significant that even before the theorists had fully developed their ideas, Thomas Gainsborough (1727–88) was improvising and imagining in his sketches and studies in pen, chalk and watercolour. He declared that for an artist to paint a landscape of any credit it "must be of his own brain". His imagination was the determining agent as he explored the pictorial possibilities of landscape. In this Gainsborough was closer to the work of the French. He may have been inspired by the drawing master Chatelain, who, it is said, piled lumps of coal on a table when drawing a rocky landscape, for Gainsborough used the same method, arranging twigs and moss in order to clarify ideas of form and composition. Such methods are indicative of the tendency towards generalization of detail and emphasis on imaginative effect that was substantiated by William Gilpin.

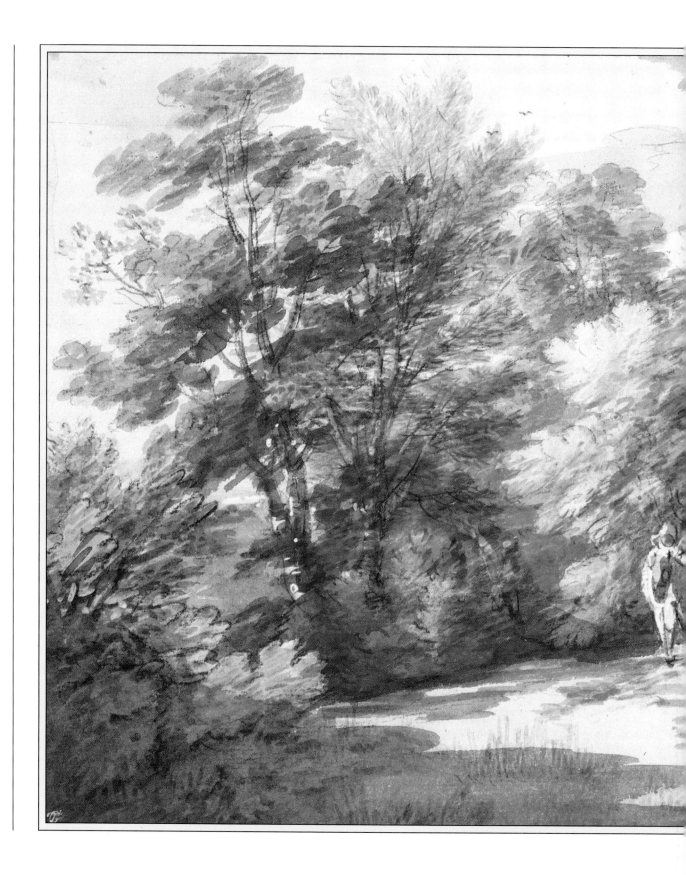

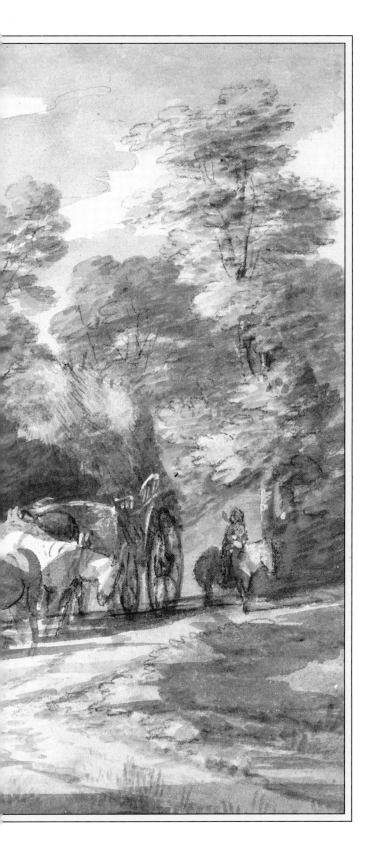

Theorists such as Gilpin and Edmund Burke, who wrote the influential *A Philosophical Enquiry into the Origin of our Ideas of the Sublime and Beautiful* (1757), were attempting to discover the fixed laws which they believed lay behind both life and art. Burke wished to formulate the rules of taste, while Gilpin set out to clarify an underlying order behind the natural scene. Both involved a process of selection and a balance of essential natural elements. Gilpin's theories provided a method by which the artist could achieve an aesthetic unity, which would in turn evoke an aesthetic response; this, at last, allowed landscapes painted in watercolour to be considered a subject worthy of the attention of both patron and connoisseur.

Notions of the Picturesque were further developed by writers such as Uvedale Price and Archibald Alison. Price evolved a theory of the historical significance of the Picturesque; the viewer's historical imagination would be kindled by "broken tints" and "rugged outlines", evidence of the passing of time. Alison in his *Essays upon the Nature and Principles of Taste* (1790) develops the theme:

Whatever increases this exercise or employment of the Imagination, increases also the emotion of Beauty and Sublimity. This is very obviously the effect of all Associations. There is no man, who has not some interesting associations with particular scenes . . . who does not feel their beauty and sublimity enhanced to him, by such connections. The view of the house where one was born, the school where one was educated . . . is indifferent to no man . . . The scenes which have been distinguished by the residence of any person, whose memory we admire, produce a similar effect . . . The scenes themselves may be little beautiful, but the delight with which we recollect . . . their lives, blends itself indefinitely with the emotions which the scenery itself, excites; . . . and converts everything to beauty which appears to have been connected with them.

Alison's aesthetic, based on "Association" and the "emotions of Taste", required a state of intense emotional activity combined with physical passivity. It revitalized the topographical-antiquarian tradition, as embodied by John Robert Cozens and John Varley.

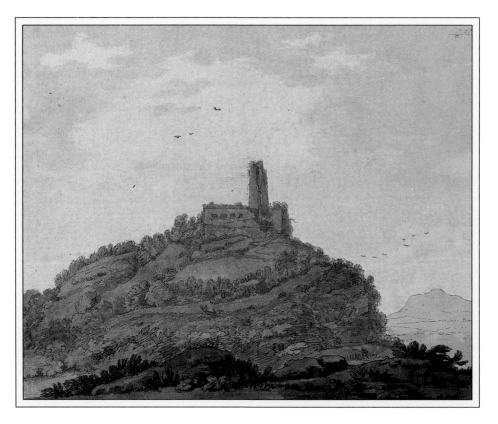

ALEXANDER COZENS: 'THE BLOTMASTER'

Before turning to examine the watercolours of John Robert Cozens, it is perhaps instructive to understand something of the work of his father, the painter Alexander Cozens (1717–86), known as 'the Blotmaster'.

Alexander Cozens' nickname resulted from his technique of 'blotting', the theory of which he expounded in *A New Method of Assisting the Invention in Drawing Original Compositions of Landscape*, published about 1786. The only complete copy of this interesting book resides in the British Museum in London. Cozens hit on the blot method by accident: while sketching on a stained piece of paper, he found himself incorporating the form of the stain into the composition. This led him to deliberately create blots and stains, tracing them onto varnished paper for use in the final drawing. A similar method of stimulating the imagination had been used by Leonardo, whose images of fantastic rocks and swirling rivers were often suggested by his observation of the shapes made by stains on the wall; the Surrealists, particularly Max Ernst, went on to develop this method in the 20th century. Cozens

A B O V E Ruins on a Hill – *Alexander Cozens. The 'blot' technique of watercolour drawing developed by him influenced many young artists, particularly his son, JR Cozens.*

claimed his technique to be superior to that of Leonardo, for he did not rely entirely on chance: "A blot is a production of chance, with a small degree of design; for in making it, the attention of the performer must be employed on the whole, or general form of the composition, and upon this only". He insisted that from the very beginning of the work the artist should have a definite idea in his mind, which must be kept continually in view. Technically, the essential characteristic of Cozens' method was 'formal' and 'suggestive' as opposed to the 'linear' technique favoured by many topographers. He writes:

> To blot, is to make varied spots or shapes with ink on paper, producing accidental forms without lines, from which ideas are presented to the mind. This is conformable to nature; for in nature forms are not distinguished by lines, but by shade and colour. To sketch is to delineate ideas; blotting suggests them.

"THE GREATEST GENIUS THAT EVER TOUCHED LANDSCAPE": JOHN ROBERT COZENS

John Robert Cozens (1752–97) owed much of his technical skill to his father's training (a little book of compositions by Alexander Cozens, which was made for the instruction of his son, is in the possession of the British Museum). Father and son were also both associated with William Beckford of Fonthill, a leading protagonist of the trend towards sensibility of feeling in late 18th-century English life. John Robert Cozens occupies a unique place in the history of watercolour. For the first time, topographic representation took second place; Cozens was more concerned with the expression of his dramatic and poetic vision than with the exact representation of a particular scene. He used watercolour for its own sake, exploiting the medium's unique expressive potential. The work of Cozens was extremely influential on the young Turner and Girtin; as students, they copied his drawings at the house of Cozens' patron, Dr Monro. Ruskin said of Cozens:

> There were two men associated with Turner in early study, who showed high promise in the same field, Cozens and Girtin (especially the former) and there is no saying what these men might have done had they lived; there might, perhaps, have been a struggle between one or other of them and Turner, as between Giorgione and Titian.

Constable owned a number of works by Cozens, enthusiastically dubbing him "the greatest genius that ever touched landscape", and admiring the "poetry", "spirit" and "sentiment" of his work.

Cozens made his first journey abroad in 1776, accompanied by the archaeologist and art collector, Richard Payne Knight, then a young dilettante of 26. The expedition lasted a year and encompassed the mountains of Switzerland and the valleys of Northern Italy. The drawings which Cozens made are mainly in monochrome, done in outline with a broad reed pen and exhibiting a loose, free handling in which the influence of Alexander Cozens is clearly apparent. In 1782 John Robert Cozens undertook his second excursion, this time in the company of William Beckford. The journey was made in luxury, with several carriages, led horses and grooms. They visited such towns as Cologne, Innsbruck, Padua, Verona, Venice, Ferrara and Naples, where both Beckford and Cozens suffered from malarial fever. The resultant sketches, produced in pencil or Indian ink, were on Cozens' return to

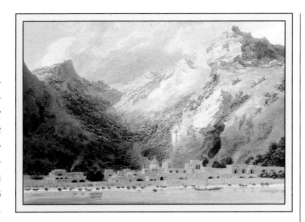

A B O V E Cetera, a Fishing Town on the Gulf of Salerno – *John Robert Cozens, 1782. JR Cozens was one of the first in Britain to use watercolours expressively, to produce works to rival the status of oils.*

England, worked up into large-scale drawings and watercolours. This accounts for the continual recurrance of certain themes in Cozens' work (a favourite subject was *The Lake of Nemi*).

Cozens rarely painted an English landscape; the majority of his work depicts the grandeur of the Italian Lakes and the Swiss Alps. He was the first English watercolourist to interpret the 'emotion' of the mountains in a personal and subjective manner, and adopted a technique whereby elements of monumentality and dignity were emphasized at the expense of obtruding detail. Even in the sunny atmosphere of the Italian plains, he continued to use tones of warm and cool blues and greys, from grey-green to pure blue. In his later work Cozens developed a technique of applying watercolour directly on to white paper, rather than adding local colour over a monochrome ground; this is demonstrated in his *View on the Galleria di Sopra, above the Lake of Albano*. Cozens' palette was deliberately restricted; he achieved his effects of sunlight and shadow by an extremely subtle manipulation of nuances of greys and blues. To achieve an effect it is often advisable to experiment with restricted means, pushing these to their limit. Indeed, as a fellow artist in watercolours, Edward Dayes wrote:

> One great inconvenience the student labours under arises from the too great quantity of colours put into his hands; an evil so encouraged by the drawing-master and colour-man, that it is not uncommon to give two or three dozen colours in a box, a thing quite unnecessary.

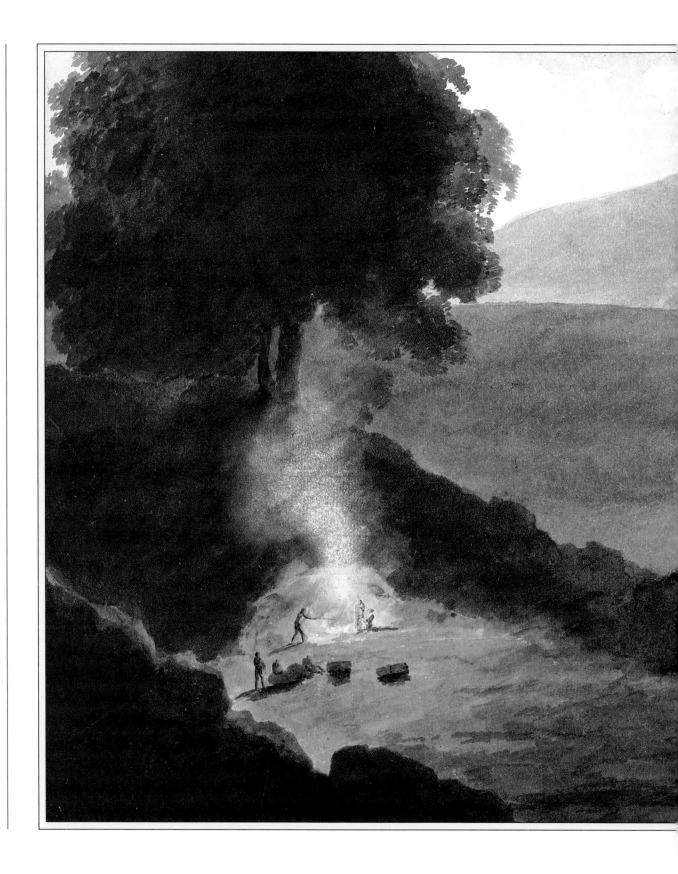

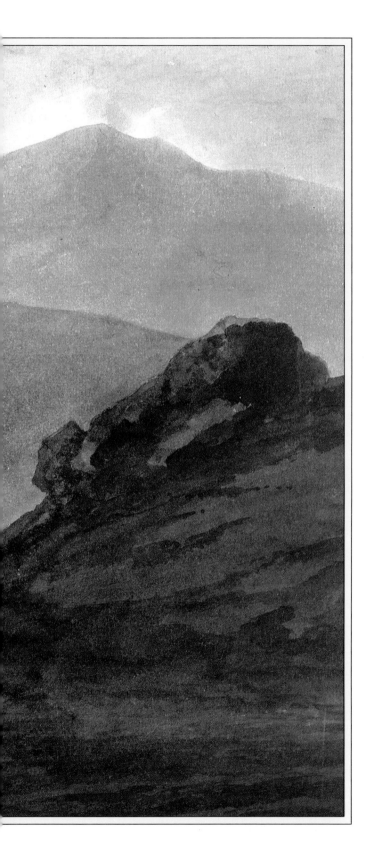

....
L E F T Between Sallanches and Servon,
Mont Blanc in the Distance – *John Robert
Cozens. The watercolours of JR Cozens were
distinguished by their poetic and spiritual
qualities; Constable termed him 'the greatest
genius that ever touched landscape'.*
....

Unlike his contemporaries, Cozens was not interested in anecdotal detail or artifice. His subject was air and space, the actuality of landscape: mountain, rock and wood, seen through the trembling light and atmosphere in which they were veiled. In his *Mountains on the Isle of Elba* his subject is as much the great expanse of sky as the ground below; his greatest skill lay in his understanding and management of light. The melancholy atmosphere which pervades Cozens' work is perhaps indicative of his later unhappy mental state; after a great deal of nervous illness he eventually became insane shortly before his death in 1797.

BRITISH ARTISTS ABROAD

Before leaving the area of landscape it is important to examine the work of a number of artists whose work was more strongly located in the topographic tradition, yet who made an important contribution to the development of the watercolour: William Pars, Francis Towne (1738–1826) and John 'Warwick' Smith (1749–1831). William Pars, ten years older than John Robert Cozens, was influential on the latter's style in both his characteristic restraint of colour and his early preference for Alpine views. In 1764 Pars was commissioned by the newly-formed Dilettanti Society to accompany an expedition to Greece and Asia Minor, areas rich in the remains of Ionian civilisation. Classical antiquity had become extremely fashionable in 18th-century English society, largely due to the work of James 'Athenian' Stuart and Nicholas Revett, whose *Antiquities of Athens* was published in 1762. The drawings made by Pars were engraved in *Ionian Antiquities* (1769 and 1797). Initially Pars' drawings tended to be rather delicate and weak, but during his second journey abroad his work began to show an increased strength characteristic of his later style. A prevailing use of gouache, the darks often varnished over, in conjunction with transparent greys and browns or greens and yellows, becomes evident in such works as *Mer de Glace, Chamouny*. His drawings of the Swiss landscape anticipate the work of Towne and Cozens, being perhaps, as Binyon calls them 'the earliest revelation of the high Alps to the untravelled English'.

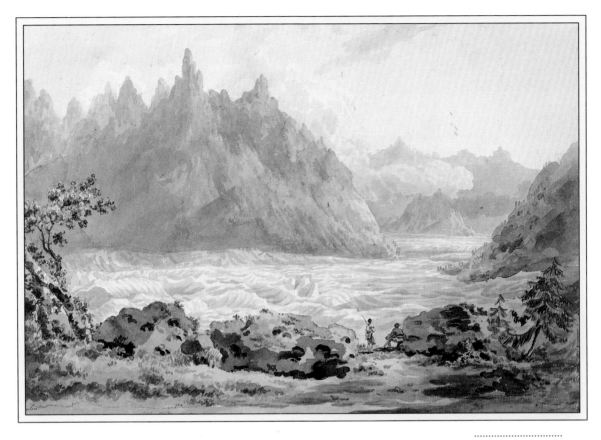

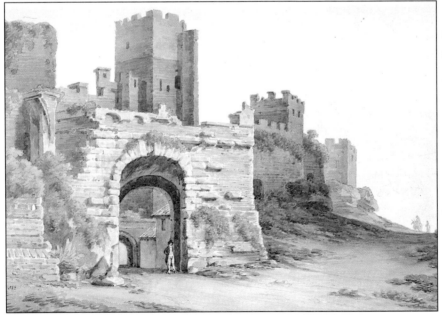

A B O V E Mer de Glace, Charmourny – *William Pars. Pars was first sent to paint abroad by the Dilettante Society, for whom he worked in Greece from 1764 to 1766. His work in Switzerland, before 1771, reveals his acute perception of the grandeur of the surrounding mountain scenery.*

L E F T Porta Tiburtina (now Porta di San Lorenzo), Rome, seen inside – *John 'Warwick' Smith. John 'Warwick' Smith forms a link between William Pars and Francis Towne, and was Towne's friend and rival. The three no doubt worked together in Switzerland or in Italy, each absorbing the influence of the other, and developing his own method and style.*

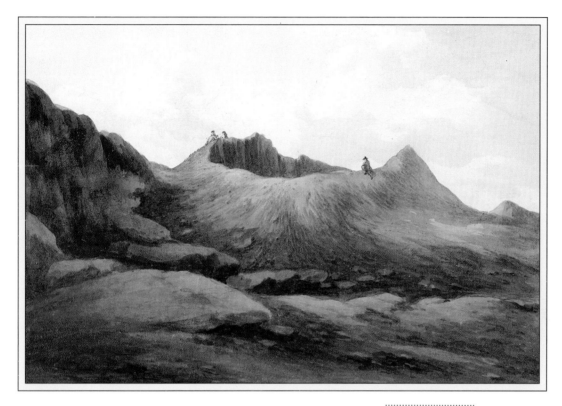

....
A B O V E The Crater Vesuvius – *John 'Warwick' Smith, 1778. A watercolour produced during Smith's period in Italy (1776–1781). He was sometimes described as 'Italian' Smith, due to his large output of Italian subjects.*
....

Pars came to an untimely end in 1782, as a letter from his friend James Irvine reveals:

> We have all been in very great grief for the loss of William Pars, who was a very robust, hearty fellow. At Tivoli he was so imprudent as to stand in the water to make a drawing, and in returning to town was seized with a kind of aguish complaint and oppression on his heart, and in a few days he died of suffocation . . . Poor fellow, I believe he was not very anxious about life, and enjoyed but little happiness in this world.

Pars' work, at its best, conveyed a feeling of spaciousness; he employed a technique of line and wash in a masterly manner to suggest the receding planes of a distant landscape. Francis Towne had a tremendous admiration for Pars, even requesting on his deathbed that his own drawings of Rome should be bequeathed to the British Museum along with those done by his friend Pars.

Another artist, John 'Warwick' Smith forms a link between Pars and Towne. Smith studied in Italy for five years, supported by the young Lord Warwick, a great admirer of his work. In Rome he was probably in close contact with Pars, who lived there from 1775 until his death in 1782, and also with Towne, who travelled with him through Switzerland in 1781. Pars and Towne were close friends and the three no doubt went sketching together, each absorbing from and influencing the other. In 1792 Smith's *Select Views of Italy* was published, illustrated by engravings. Much has been recorded of Smith's technique. WH Pyne again writes:

> It is due to this ingenius draughtsman of the old school, to assign to him the credit of being the first who successfully aimed at producing that force in water-colours, which assumed the appearance of a picture, properly so designated, some of his Italian scenery, although the *chiaroscuro* was prepared with grey, being tinted almost up to the force of oil painting. To use the phrase of Gainsborough, Smith was the first professor of water-colour art, who had 'carried his intention through'. His most successful works, though not many in number, certainly surpassed in the union of light, shadow, and colour, all that had been produced before.

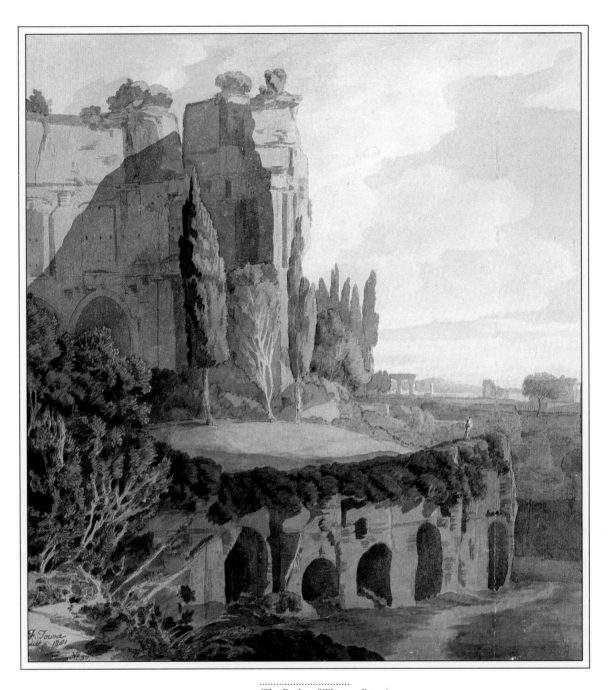

A B O V E The Baths of Titus — *Francis
Towne. As with many other watercolourists of
this period, Towne found new inspiration for his
work in the landscapes of Italy; his reputation
rests largely on the drawings he produced abroad.*

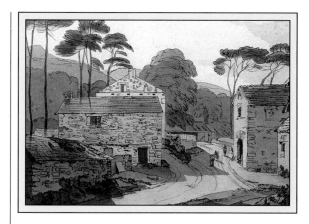

Despite such laudatory accounts, Smith was not a technical innovator, but was following in a tradition, as did many of the earlier watercolourists; even Girtin hovered between a traditional and a more advanced technique. Above all, an examination of Smith's work reveals the influence of his friend Francis Towne, an artist who, during his own life-time, received almost no recognition.

Towne's obscurity was partly due to his own personality; he once boasted that he had never exhibited a drawing in his life, although this is perhaps a result of his lower estimation of the watercolour medium in contrast to oil. Towne worked largely in oils, with rather negligible success.; he used watercolour primarily as a basis for oil painting, engraving, or purely for his own pleasure. The chief quality of Towne's approach to watercolour was the emphasis he gave to structure, pattern and design while simplifying form. His drawings, with their delicate outlines and refined compositions of subdued, flat colour washes, had little appeal for a generation whose ideas of artistic excellence were shaped by the high drama of Poussin and Claude. It was not until the early 20th century, when European eyes became accustomed to the refinements of Japanese art, that Towne's work received the true acclaim it deserved.

The first drawings which demonstrate his powerful originality were made on a sketching tour of Wales in 1777 and 1778. Towne made a whole series of numbered and dated sketches, often done on the double sheet of a sketchbook. On the reverse of many of these are noted the orders for copies in watercolour or for paintings in oil. His method was to make an outline pencil sketch on the spot, and afterwards go over the outline in ink, washing on the colour while the memory of the scene was still fresh in his mind. Towne was one of the first artists to realize that the mountain scenery of Britain was a worthy subject for the artist's brush; and he depicted it through his own experience rather than through the intermediary influence of Italianates such as Poussin or Rosa.

It was during a tour to Rome in 1780–1781 that Towne, his imagination heightened by the spectacular scenery around him, began to produce some of the best work of his career. In all, he completed 74 Italian drawings, collected together in three volumes, now held in the British Museum. Towne resided with his friend William Pars, whose influence may be discerned in Towne's Roman watercolours; Towne was perhaps also influenced by the work of John Robert Cozens, who had only shortly before left Rome for England. In contrast to that of his friends. Towne's work is distinguished by its sharpness of focus and by his ability to enhance the dramatic effect of his image by careful cropping. A striking example is his *Baths of Caracalla*, in which he demonstrates his use of delicate outline in conjunction with a simple massing of low, rich areas of tone; *The Temple of Vesta, The Baths of Titus* and *L'Arricia* are all good examples of the same effect.

On his return to England, in the company of John 'Warwick' Smith, Towne passed through the Swiss Alps. It was a formative experience, for Towne's Swiss drawings are undoubtedly his finest work. His ability to realize structure and simplify mass found an ideal subject in the grandeur of the mountain scenery. His vision can only be described as sublime; as Oppe writes "contrary to all the accepted canons of the 18th century, Towne did nothing to soften, but everything to accentuate the crushing grandeur of the mountains". In works such as *The Source of the Arveyron* he conveys his sense of awe before the might of nature through a carefully designed, formal composition, which is more forceful for its restrained colour.

In his emphasis on structure and his bold simplification of form, Towne anticipated the masters of the 20th century. As Oppe says:

Towne's special skill lies in the management of even pen line and in subtle modulation of colour upon a flat surface. The one gives variation and tone to his large imaginative patterning, the other a charm and delicacy which vary but do not weaken it.

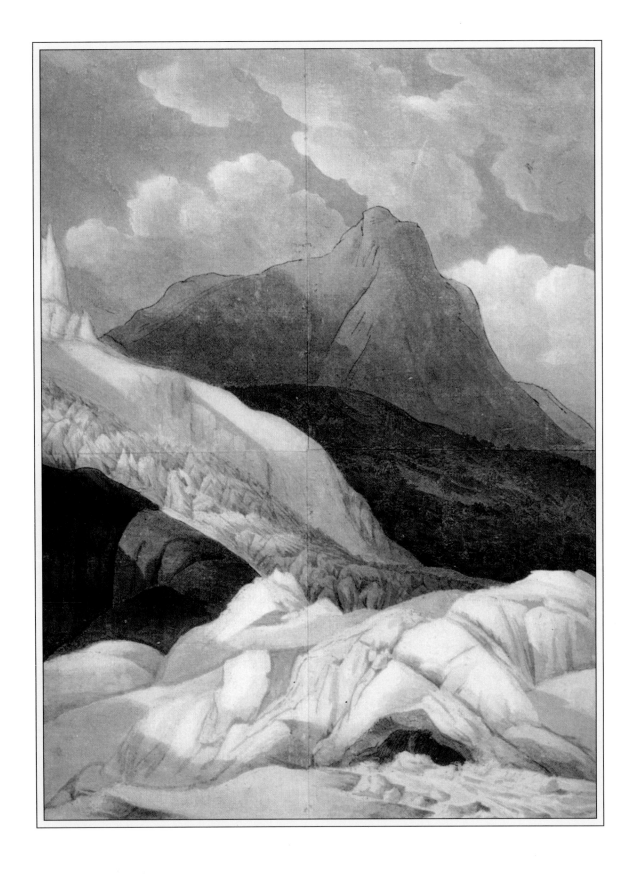

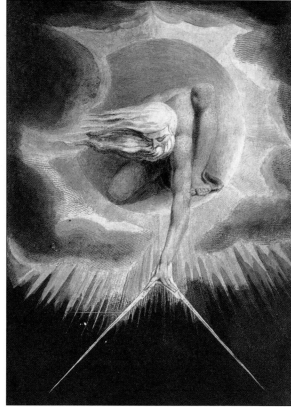

BLAKE AND FUSELI:
VISIONARY AND ROMANTIC

Two painters who stood outside the mainstream of art during the late 18th century were William Blake (1757–1827) and Henry Fuseli (1741–1825). Both were powerful, imaginative artists who turned away from the tradition of representational painting and instead transcribed their inner visions, inspired by Bible themes and the literary works of Homer, Dante and Milton. Though little appreciated in their own lifetime, the mystical, dreamlike images of Blake and Fuseli were to exert a great influence on the work of the 20th-century Surrealists.

The talents of William Blake were numerous: as a painter, poet, philosopher, engraver and illustrator, the diversity of his work makes him extremely hard to categorize as an artist. Above all, he stands alone as one who was not only possessed of an extraordinary inner vision, but had the power and ability to communicate that vision through the medium of art.

After an early training in drawing, the young Blake was apprenticed to the engraver James Basire. The boy had already begun to form his own collection of prints, including reproductions of Michelangelo's work; the artist was to remain a lifelong influence on Blake's own work. With Basire, Blake became fully versed in all the technical skills of the engraver's art. This proved formative in determining Blake's own conviction of the superior expressive merits of drawing, in particular outline, which led him to assert: "Painting is drawing on Canvas, & Engraving is drawing on Copper, & Nothing Else; he who pretends to be either Painter or Engraver without being a Master of drawing is an Imposter".

By 1788 Blake had completed his first major book of poems, *Songs of Innocence*. In order to publish this work Blake evolved a method of printing which allowed him to produce words and pictures together as a single unit. By etching 'the whites' instead of 'the blacks' – a reversal of the normal printing process – and delineating the design and text with stop-out medium. Blake was able to produce a positive image rather like a woodcut. This could then be linked up in a wide variety of colours and easily printed by hand. The prints were then tinted with watercolour, the pigments being

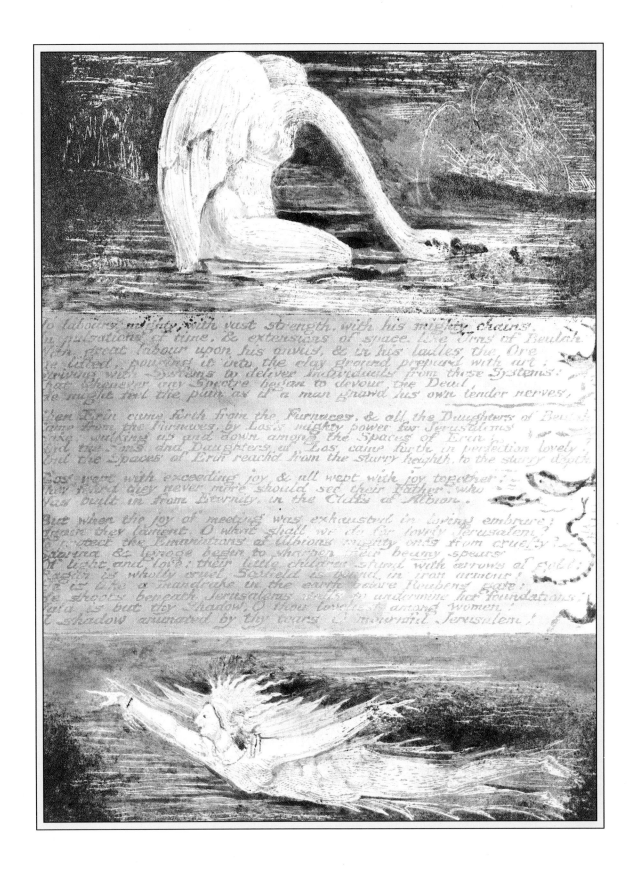

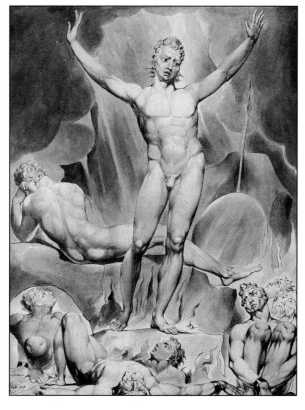

ground and mixed by Blake himself and bound by hand. Other volumes followed: *Songs of Experience, The Marriage of Heaven and Hell* and *Jerusalem*, all printed using similar techniques.

Some of Blake's most fascinating work, both from the point of view of technique and as examples of his extraordinary powers of visual realization, are the 'colour-printed drawings', the best examples of which may be seen in the collection at the Tate Gallery in London. All were executed around 1795, including such as: *Newton, Nebuchadnezzar, The Good and Evil Angels, Pity,* and *Adam,* each of which was coloured in an ever more complex and demanding manner. The technique was extremely interesting. Blake would draw out his key design on a piece of absorbent board, colour would then be added in the form of paint, bound with such a medium as egg yolk, an impression was then stamped on prepared paper. When the printing was complete, Blake would finish the process with hand additions in watercolour. This technique allowed for chance effects and produced an element of texture which could not have been achieved by more conventional methods. Blake's experimentation with technique led him to develop what he termed his 'fresco' painting.

This entailed preparing a board or canvas with a ground of whiting and glue, onto which the artist would paint using tempera or watercolour. The results may be seen in such works as *Satan Smiting Job,* in the Tate Gallery, London. Despite the wide and subtle range of printing techniques which Blake evolved, it is important to realize that when he used watercolour alone he was faithful to more traditional methods, laying tints of colour over a monochrome ground of Indian ink.

Blake's work was controversial in his day, and attracted much criticism. All his life, he worked long, hard hours as an engraver and illustrator, kept from the workhouse door solely by the support of a few far-sighted patrons. In 1808 he held a one-man exhibition, in an effort to achieve some degree of recognition for his work. Despite the enthusiasm expressed by a number of discerning critics, such as Charles Lamb, the exhibition was not the success Blake had hoped for. He struggled on until 1818, when he became acquainted with the young painter John Linnell and his friends John Varley, George Richmond, Edward Calvert and Samuel Palmer. These artists recognized Blake's genius and soon became devoted disciples.

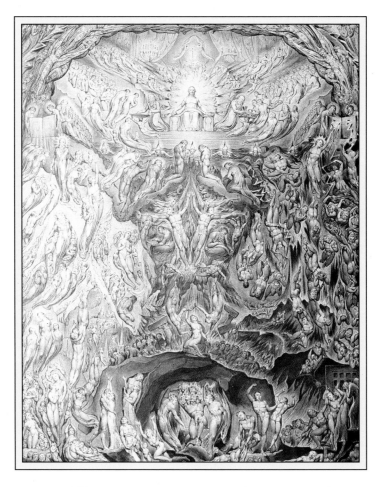

ABOVE The Last Judgement – *William Blake. Blake's extraordinary vision of Heaven and Hell.*

and his famous *The Nightmare*, reveal the skills he acquired in Rome at the service of an extraordinarily powerful imagination. Fuseli depicted his dreams and obsessions, his images fired by spectral creatures "humour", pathos, terror, blood and murder".

ROWLANDSON AND SOCIAL SATIRE

The watercolours of the social satirist Thomas Rowlandson (1756–1827) stand in complete contrast to those of Blake and Fuseli. While they were obsessed with the spiritual and the supernatural, Rowlandson was embroiled in the decidedly earthy activities of the human race. His boisterous, even bawdy caricatures reveal the hypocricies of Regency England with great energy and humour, providing an unrivalled visual document of social life at that time. Rowlandson remained aloof to new movements in watercolour art, his style and technique alerting little during his career. He was foremost in establishing the methods of Sandby

Calling themselves 'The Ancients', the group's enthusiasm revitalized the older artist's later years. They provided the sympathetic understanding and appreciation missing from Blake's earlier career, as well as important commissions, such as the illustrations to Dante's *Divine Comedy*, suggested by Linnell. Blake was working on these when he died in 1827.

Despite lack of official recognition for his work, Blake's unique imaginative, even visionary powers inspired many fellow artists, foremost among whom was his friend Henry Fuseli. The Swiss-born Fuseli settled in England in 1778, after studying for eight years in Rome, sketching the antique and absorbing the work of the Italian masters; like Blake, he revered the work of Michelangelo. Works such as *Night Hag*,

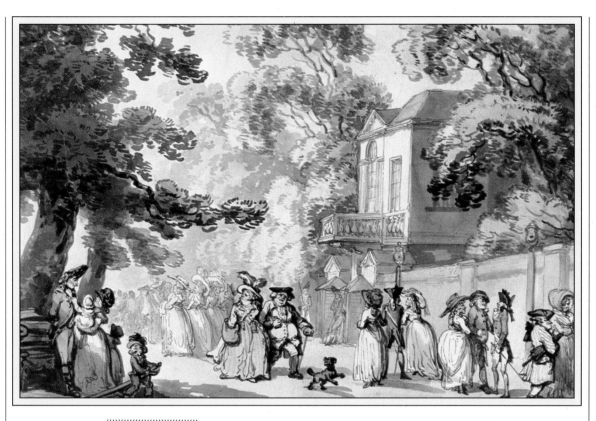

....
A B O V E Entrance to the Mall, Spring
Gardens – *Thomas Rowlandson. Rowlandson*
developed an extreme economy of line in his
drawings, for people and landscape.
....

and the topographers, applying tints of colour to pen drawing and monochrome wash. His portrayal of the more seamy and squalid aspects of life was a direct result of his own periods of dissipation. On the death of an aunt, Rowlandson received a legacy of £7,000 and thereafter became a regular frequenter of the gaming-houses of London. It is claimed that on one occasion, such was his infatuation with the dice that he continued at the gaming table nearly 36 hours. His fortune spent, and deeply in debt, Rowlandson turned to his pen, and, working furiously, went on to produce a huge annual output of prints and drawings.

Rowlandson's biting sense of humour and masterly technique are demonstrated in such works as *Exhibition Stair-Case*, which depicts the staircase at Somerset House, where the Royal Academy exhibitions were held. The foolishness of the pompous and pretentious 'culture lovers' is revealed as they tumble ignobly down the stairs, one after the other, creating a hilarious cascade of human limbs. It was Rowlandson's habit to work with a reed pen and watered ink, which facilitated extremely fluid line characteristic of his work. What Blake referred to as Rowlandson's 'bounding line' with 'its infinite' inflections and movements', is demonstrated by the composition's central, sinuous, S-shaped curve of activity. Colour, as always, is limited, the subtle harmonies contained within the boundaries of the drawn outlines; Rowlandson relied on his economic and vibrant line to convey the full expressive force of his work.

THE WATERCOLOUR IN EUROPE

While, in Britain, watercolour became progressively established as an art form in its own right, in Europe, where it had initially flourished, its use and consequent development were more sporadic. In Holland, artists produced a diverse range of work in the medium. Cornelis Troost (1697–1750) painted sumptuous studies of fruit and flowers, flooding the colour directly onto the paper. The increased number of British visitors to Italy, as a result of the Grand Tour, provided many artists with work, creating a tradition of English patronage of Italian draughtsmanship. Giovanni Battista

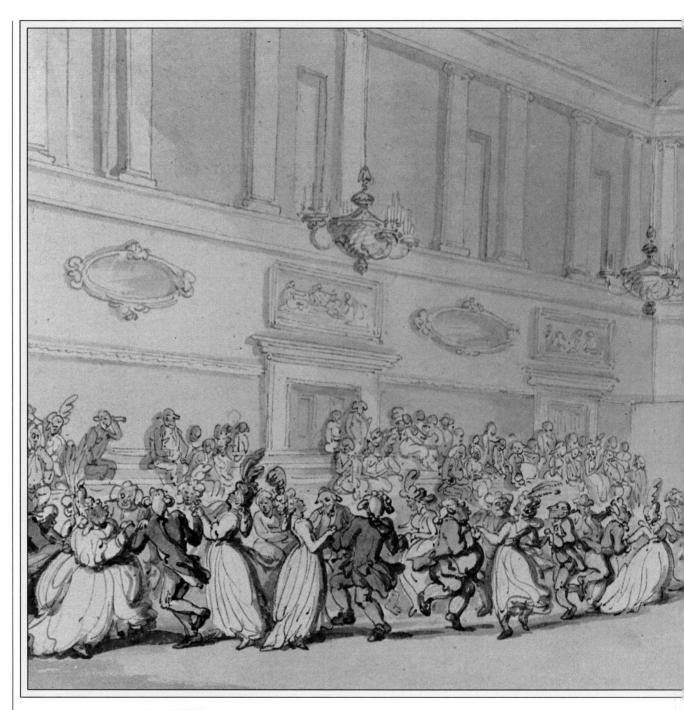

....
ABOVE **La Salle de Bal, Bath –** *Thomas*
Rowlandson. Thomas Rowlandson was one of
the great masters of line. His brilliant caricatures
provide us with a unique insight into the social
manners and modes of Regency England.
....

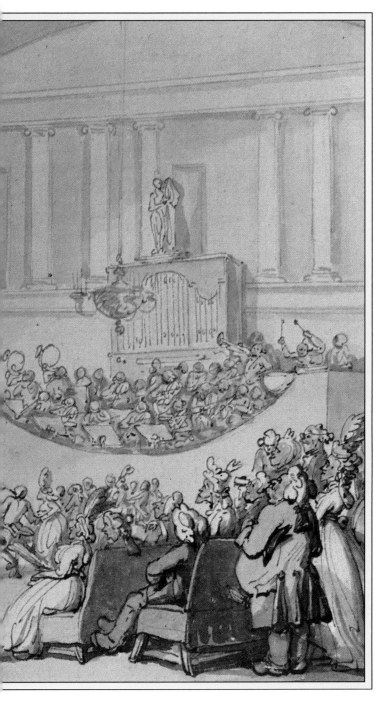

Busiri's scenes near Rome were collected by William Windham; in Venice, Marco Ricci painted landscapes and ruins in the unusual medium of tempera on leather, while Canaletto worked in pen and wash.

The word *aquarelle*, for watercolour, was not introduced into France until 1775; previously, no distinction was made between watercolour and gouache. At first, watercolour was not a medium generally used by recognized artists, other than for their own preparatory drawings and sketches. Its use by enthusiastic amateurs did, however, increase rapidly. Some of the most interesting watercolours of the early part of the century were illustrations of costume designs by Henry Gissey, who created the dresses for the Royal Ballets of Louis XIV. The fashion for delicacy of style, reflecting the enormous popularity of the rococo, encouraged artists to work as draughtsmen, producing book illustrations, engravings and highly decorated luxury items.

One such example is Moreau le Jeune's famous designs for *Le Monument du Costume* of the 1770s. Such artists as Gabriel de Saint-Aubin produced beautifully delicate watercolours depicting the elegance and sophistication of Parisian life, while Niklas Lavrience produced intimate scenes with erotic overtones drawn on ivory or vellum.

Landscape painting came back into fashion and rural life became romanticized; the innocent idyll of nature was an escape from the harsh realities of the urban environment. Artists took to the technique of sketching outdoors, *sur le motif*, and the landscape and antiquities of Rome became especially popular themes. A number of artists began to work consistently in watercolour, for instance Louis-Jean Desprez, who spent the early part of his career in Italy and the latter part in Sweden. His distinctive style embodied a lively use of line and local colour. Other notable artists who gathered in Rome were the Swiss, Abraham Ducros and the German, Philipp Hackert. The former developed a method of producing large, forceful watercolours, powerful enough to be framed alongside oils; he rarely sold the originals, preferring to use them as a basis for engravings. The latter was renowned for his social evenings, at which amateurs would practise the art of sketching, and his opinions on art were extremely influential. Rome acted as a meeting place for artists of all nationalities; inspired by the classical-Arcadian ruins of their ancient past, they would exchange technical theories and develop ideas, thereby hastening the evolution of both European art in general and the watercolour in particular.

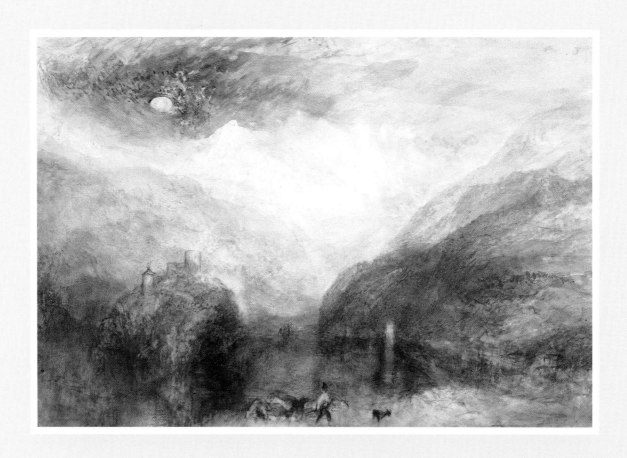

CHAPTER THREE

THE 19th CENTURY

OPPOSITE **View of the Lake of Brienz** – *Joseph Mallord William Turner. Fascinated by the mysterious and elemental forces of nature, artists in the 19th century capitalized on watercolour's ability to create subtle tonal variations that captured nuances of light and atmosphere.*

By the time of Cozens' death in 1797, a significant group of new artists was coming to the fore in England, artists who have profoundly influenced how we see and experience nature today. Renaissance conventions were at last being replaced by a more personal, less academic response to the visual world. The new generation of painters confronted nature 'in the raw' with an awe and reverance for its mysterious and elemental forces. Working from direct observation, they recorded spontaneous and intimate responses to the countryside, rather than attempting to copy, idealize or formalize it, as artists of the 17th and 18th centuries had done. This fundamental change was described by the artist James Patterson:

> Absolute truth to nature was impossible. A selection from and suggestion of the tones and tints and forms which we saw in the landscape was the only course open to the painter. What might be called decoration was an essential quality of every real work of art . . . It thus arose that in nearly all the greatest examples of landscape there was a distinct departure from the actual facts of nature, a departure wilful and necessary, and not accidental and culpable.

Landscape painters in the early 19th century often turned to watercolour because, best of all media, it expressed their immediate response to nature and conveyed its transient and fluctuating moods. The ease and weightlessness of watercolour allowed artists to develop their poetic ideas; brushstrokes could leap across the paper, and washes of colour could fuse into semblances of water, clouds, trees and mountains. Seeking to create 'impressions' of nature, rather than a precise representation, they developed a watercolour technique, today considered the classic English style, in which thin, transparent washes were built up, layer upon layer, to achieve a luminous transparency.

The traditional 'linear' description of landscapes soon lost favour as artists explored the emotional effects of colour and watercolour's ability to create infinitely subtle tonal variations that captured nuances of light and atmosphere. "When the tones are right, the lines draw themselves", proclaimed the champion of the Romantic spirit, Delacroix.

....
OPPOSITE Landscape with a church beside a river – *Thomas Girtin. A friend and contemporary of Turner, Thomas Girtin specialized in watercolour and in his short life revolutionized landscape painting in that medium.*
....

GIRTIN AND THE BRITISH TRADITION

Thomas Girtin (1775–1802) died at the early age of 27, a victim of asthma, weakened by a life of hard and honest work. His premature death meant the loss of one of the greatest British painters in watercolour. Turner, Girtin's fellow student and life-long friend, is said to have exlaimed "Had poor Tom had lived, I should have starved".

Girtin and Turner were extremely close. Only two months separated them in age, and they were born on opposite sides of the Thames. Girtin the son of a rope-maker, Turner the son of a barber. Despite this proximity they were of the most opposite characters conceivable: "Girtin open, vivacious, generous and joyous; Turner close, inscrutable and taciturn" (Binyon). The young men first met as apprentices, employed in colouring prints and 'laying in' washes for architects. An important early figure for both was Dr Monro, who patronised young artists, providing them with employment and encouraging their work. For Monro Girtin made topographic drawings for magazines and copies from the Italian drawings of Cozens. The effect on Girtin's artistic development was immense. Around 1796 Girtin suddenly developed into an interpreter of nature as opposed to a topographical draughtsman, a mere recorder of nature; it was after this date that Girtin broke away from Turner and developed a distinct manner of his own.

Girtin turned away from traditional methods to develop a vision and technique that was to completely change the character of British watercolour. Mayne writes: "Not one characteristic English watercolour of the early 19th century could be imagined without presupposing Girtin". The most outstanding example of this new method is *The White House at Chelsea*. It displays a new conception of watercolour in its broad and simple design and exceptional subtlety of tone, combined with the daring of sudden contrast. When a dealer viewing Turner's work claimed to have seen something finer, Turner replied, "I don't know what that can be unless it's Tom Girtin's *White House at Chelsea*". This new vision was the result of Girtin's adoption of a number of novel techniques, the most important of which was his abandonment of grey underpainting, thus allowing light to reflect off the white of the paper and give the watercolour washes their full and transparent brilliance. He also abandoned the practice of drawing preliminary outlines in

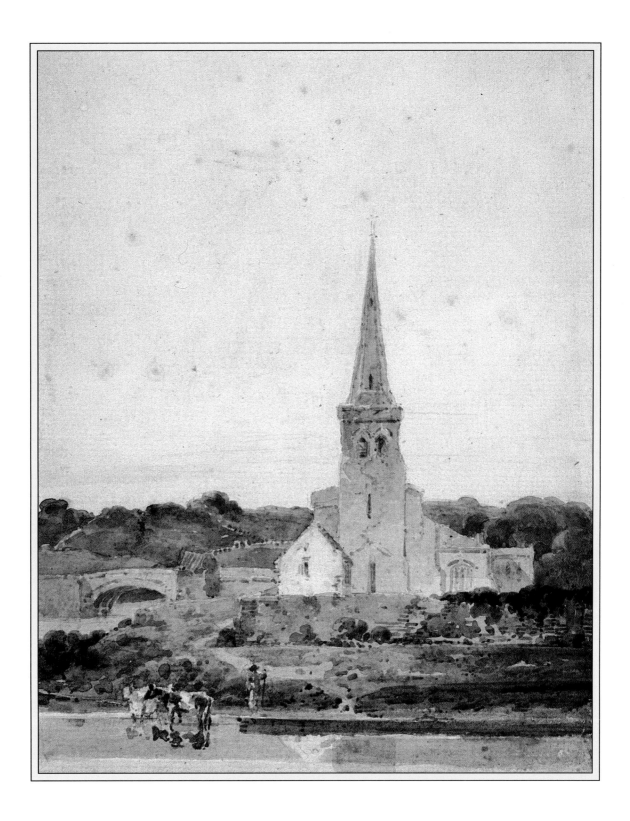

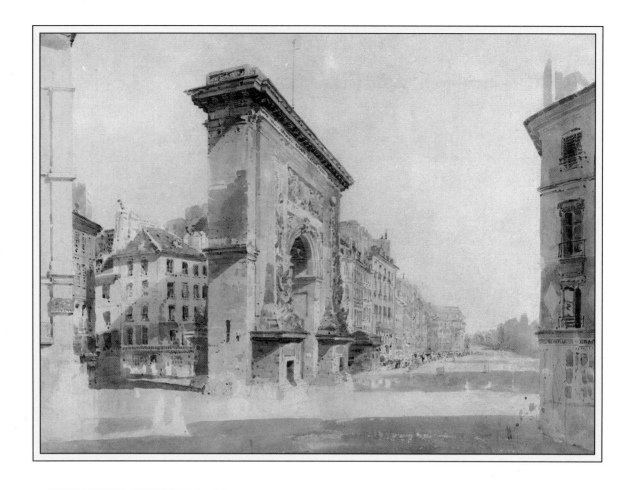

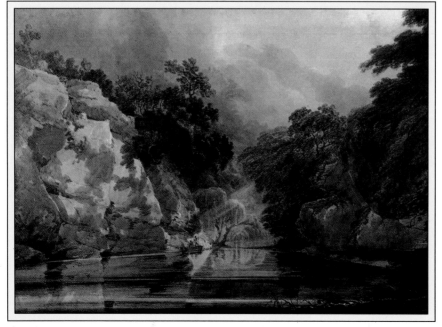

A B O V E Porte Saint-Denis, Paris – *Thomas Girtin. Favouring coarse cartridge paper, Girtin abandoned grey underpainting and allowed light to reflect off the surface of the paper to give added brilliance to his work.*

L E F T Plumpton Rocks, near Knaresborough – *Thomas Girtin. With hardly a care for adverse conditions, Girtin would set out to record the momentary effects of light and weather.*

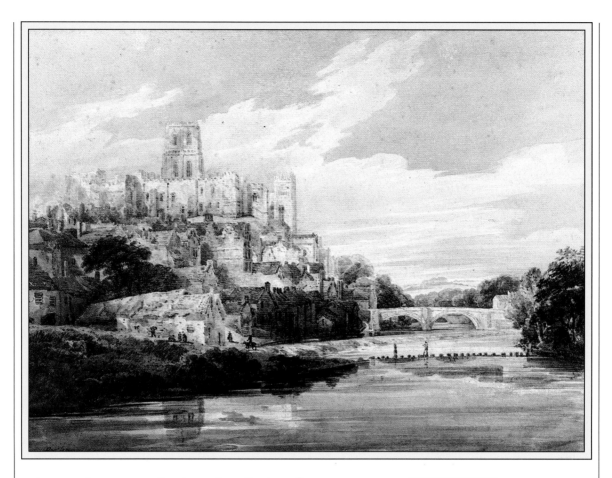

order to gain a greater freedom of application of colour. WH Pyne writes:

> (Girtin) prepared his drawings on the same principle which had hitherto been confined to painting in oil, namely, laying in the object upon his paper, with the local colour, and shadowing the same with the individual tint of its own shadow.

Organization of tone and value was also fundamental to Girtin's method; Pyne continues:

> When he had accomplished the laying in of his sky, he would proceed with great facility in the general arrangement of his tints, on the buildings, trees, water, and other objects. Every colour appeared to be placed with a most judicious perception to effecting a general union or harmony.

Girtin's choice of paper was also innovative; most watercolourists used a slightly absorbent paper, made from linen rags, on which the colour settled without hard edges. Girtin favoured a coarse cartridge, with slight blemishes which gave variety and texture to the surface, and of a warmish tint which, left untouched

A B O V E Durham Cathedral and Castle –
Thomas Girtin. Girtin's sky, strong in colour and cold in tone contrasts with the warm, rich tones of the land.

in parts, gave his work a low, harmonious tonality. His palette was extremely limited, no more than six or seven colours being used in any one drawing. He drew with the brush, obliterating outlines in a broad fusion of colour, light and form. Skies were always an important feature, strong in colour and often cold in tone, in contrast with the warm, rich tones of his landscape. Girtin was one of the first to capture the momentary effects of light and weather, conveying a real feeling of atmosphere. Many of his watercolours were made before nature; with hardly a care for bad weather he would sit out to observe the effect of storms and clouds.

Girtin's major achievement was to work in accordance with his own experience before nature; he opened the way for artists to interpret their own sensations, rather than simply follow accepted rules.

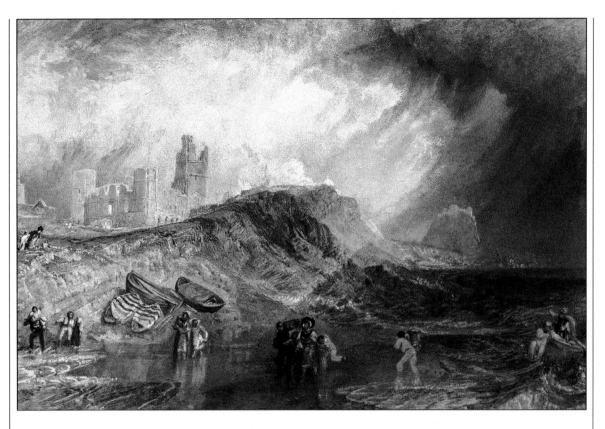

JOSEPH MALLORD WILLIAM TURNER

The only other artist who really surpassed Girtin was Turner (1775–1851), and this was perhaps due to his far longer working life; in 1802, Turner was elected a member of the Royal Academy. While Girtin felt free to interpret nature, Turner went a step further; always ready to alter and invent, he superimposed his own ideas on nature, the better to express his visions of drama and motion. Turner frequently made sketching tours around Britain and much of Europe. On a tour through Switzerland in 1802 he made over 400 land-scape in Romantic fashion, often depicting the vast-ness and grandeur of nature. The majority of these were in bodycolour on paper prepared with a grey wash, which enabled him to work rapidly outdoors. On a later Italian tour he relied mainly upon pencil sketches, of which he produced no less than 1,500 in six months. Turner was in demand for popular topo-graphical views, many of which were engraved for magazines and illustrated albums. He accumulated notes in his sketchbooks, many of which would turn up in finished watercolours years later.

A B O V E Richmond, Yorkshire – *Joseph Mallord William Turner. On sketching tours in Britain and Europe, Turner depicted the vastness and grandeur of nature.*

R I G H T A Barn: Interior of the Ruined Refectory of St. Martin's Priory, Dover – *Joseph Mallord William Turner.*

Turner's topographic apprenticeship had influenced the style of his early watercolours, with their cool, subdued colours and attention to detail, line and struc-ture. Increasingly, though, he became involved with the depiction of light, space and colour, and towards the end of his life he strove to capture the very essence of light. As his watercolours achieved a greater airiness and luminosity, their linear content faded and event-ually disappeared. There was a greater concern with the study of reflected light and atmospheric changes, a merging and massing of tones – and the develop-ment of a brilliantly inventive technique to convey the effects he wanted. William Leighton Leitch describes Turner at work:

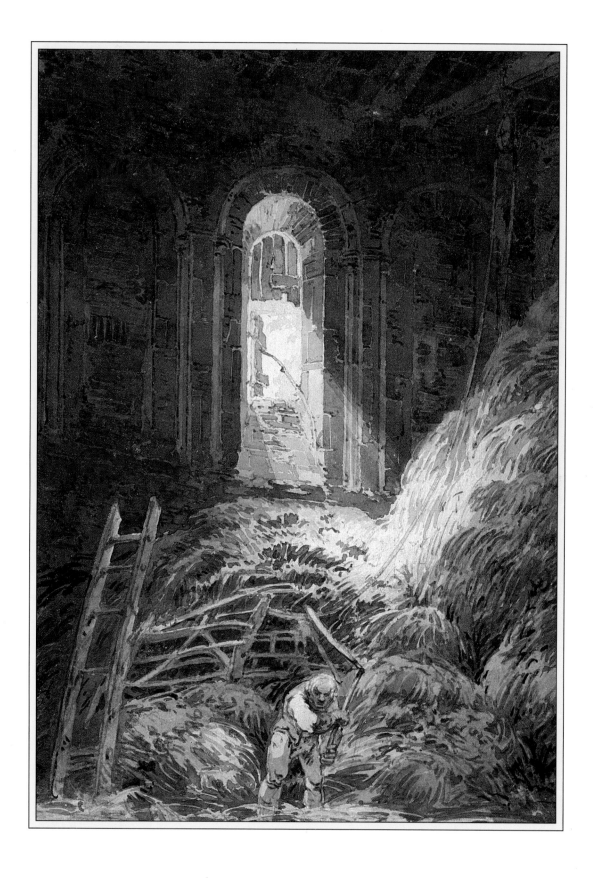

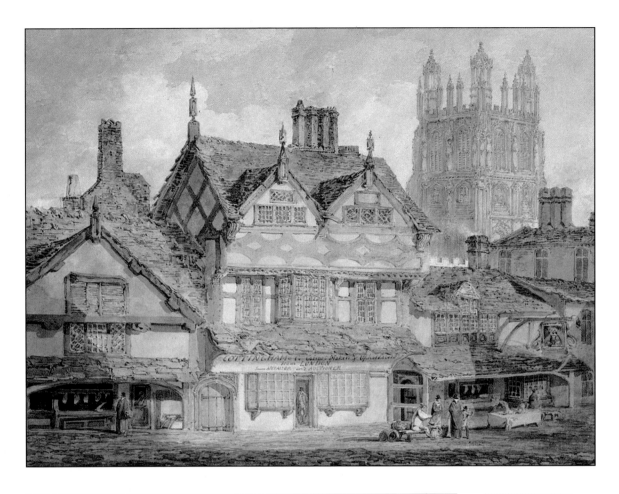

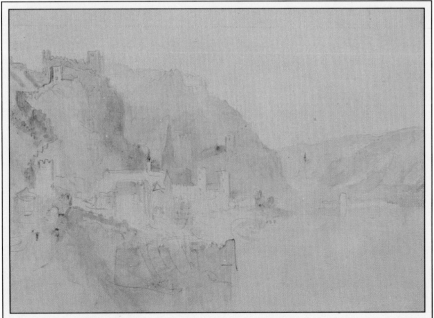

ABOVE Wrexham, Denbighshire – *Joseph Mallord William Turner.*

LEFT On The Rhine – *Joseph Mallord William Turner. In 1817 Turner painted a series of delicate watercolours from pencil sketches made on the banks of the Rhine.*

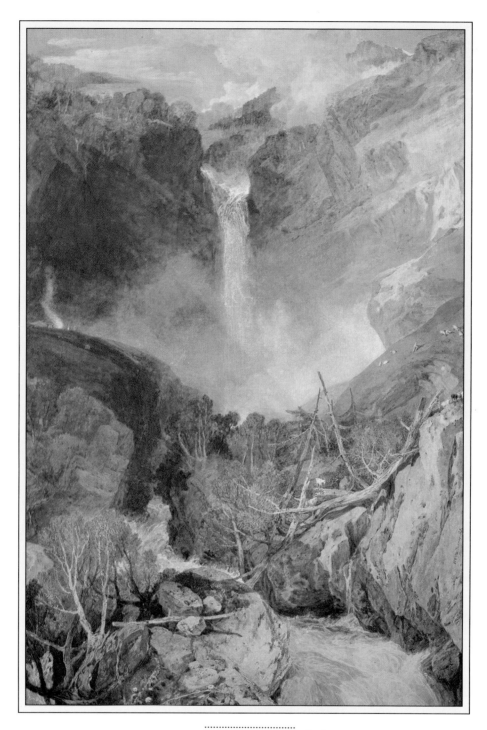

....

ABOVE Great Falls of Reichenbach –
Joseph Mallord William Turner. This
magnificent view of Alpine scenery painted for
exhibition in 1804 reveals Turner's use of
watercolour for the expression of a vast and
solemn romantic theme.

....

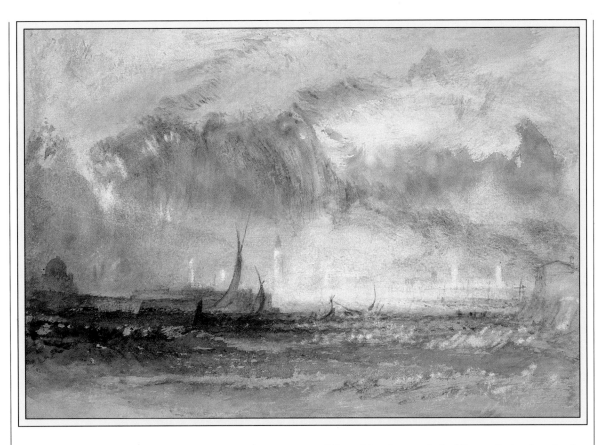

....
A B O V E Venice, Storm at Sunset – *Joseph Mallord William Turner. Attracted by the brilliance of light and low sky-line, Turner visited Venice on several occasions.*
....

". . . he dropped the colours onto the paper whilst it was still wet, making *marblings* and gradations throughout the work. His completing process was marvellously rapid, for he indicated his masses and incidents, took out half-lights, scraped out highlights and dragged, hatched and stippled until the design was finished."

Turner's response to landscape was personal and emotional, the technique he developed idiosyncratic: colour was washed down and fresh colour floated on top, lights were taken out with a wet brush, blotting paper, a rag or scraped out with a knife. He worked increasingly in stipple, breaking up areas of tone into speckles and dots, removing colour with a finely pointed wet brush. Turner became famous for his method of dragging dryish colour with the side of the brush in order to create a suggestion of broken texture; this technique was later used by such artists as Cotman and Boys. Most innovatively, Turner insisted on keying his colour to a higher and higher pitch of brightness.

Around 1835 Turner's health began to fail and he increasingly spent his time abroad; this period was his latest and purest 'spiritual' phase of watercolour. The works, from the slightest sketch to the most highly worked drawing, are visionary creations of radiant light and colour. Light became the central theme of Turner's art; it suffused land and seascapes, finally becoming more tangible than both. He used every device in his power: sponging, rubbing, washing, hatching and retouching, to convey the lyricism of light and the mystery of its reality. Throughout his long life Turner continued to experiment with and to explore the possibilities of watercolour. He was never satisfied; these words of Lytton Strachey sum up the spirit of the man:

He was a child of the Romantic Revival, a creature of emotion and of memory, a dreamer whose secret spirit dwelt apart in delectable mountains, an artist whose subtle sense caught, like a shower in the sunshine, the impalpable rainbow of the immaterial world.

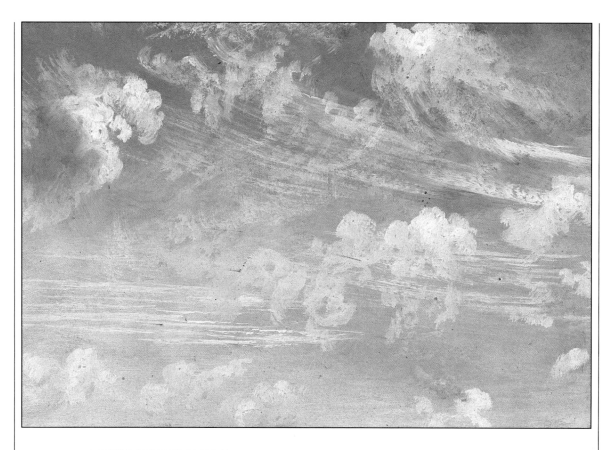

JOHN CONSTABLE: THE PAINTER OF SKIES

A B O V E Study of Cirrhus Clouds – *John Constable. John Constable revolutionized the art of watercolour, bringing to it his acute observations of weather, light and atmosphere.*

John Constable (1776–1837) was born in East Berghold, overlooking the valley of the Stour. His best work was always painted amidst the countryside of his birth, and Constable himself claimed 'Those scenes made me a painter, and I am grateful'. Throughout his life he rarely exhibited watercolours, and the importance of his work in the medium was not recognized until after his death, when a collection of over 300 sketches and drawings was given to the Victoria & Albert Museum by his daughter. These works demonstrate that Constable revolutionized the art of watercolour, bringing to it his unique understanding of nature and his acute observations of weather, light and atmosphere.

Constable devoted his whole life to landscape. In particular, he became a master of skies, writing:

> the sky is the keynote, the standard of scale, and the chief organ of sentiment . . . the sky is the source of light in nature, which governs everything.

Another major influence on the formation of Constable's style was Sir George Beaumont, who possessed a large collection of the works of the great landscape masters: Claude, Rubens, Ruisdael, Gainsborough and Girtin, which Constable would study; he remained, however, independent in his attitude to art. Beaumont insisted that "a good picture, like a good fiddle, shall be brown". In reaction, Constable laid a fiddle down on the ground to demonstrate the strength of colour in the natural landscape.

The majority of Constable's watercolours belong to the period 1826–34, during which time he produced such works as *Old Sarum in Storm, 1828*, which, even though on a tiny scale, captures an effect of light and fresh breezes. Another version of *Old Sarum in Storm* is a vibrant sketch redolent of the eerie light which comes between thunder and sun. It was Constable's habit to work with separate, vibrant touches of colour, rather in the manner of David Cox, as opposed to an even wash; he utilized a controlled looseness of colour,

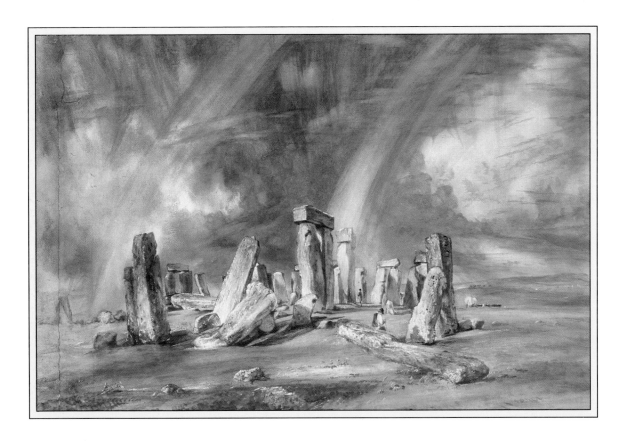

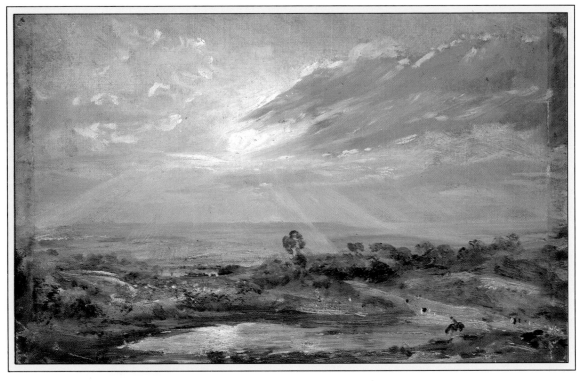

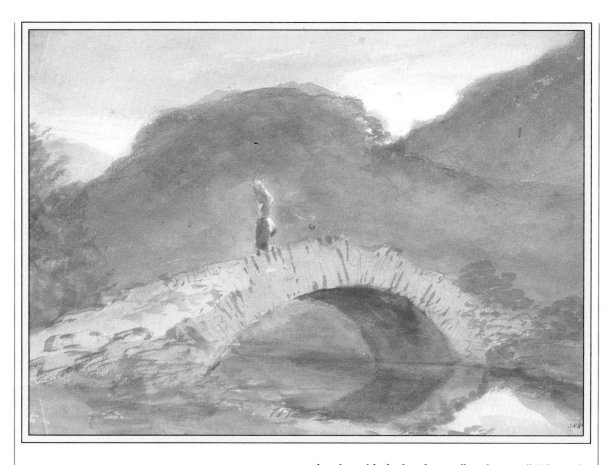

OPPOSITE ABOVE Stonehenge, Wiltshire ('The Mysterious Monument') – *John Constable. One of a series of work in and around Salisbury, this view of Stonehenge exhibits a favourite device of Constable's – that of contrasting a light foreground against a dramatic backdrop of blue sky.*

OPPOSITE BELOW Branch Hill Pond, Hampstead Sunset – *John Constable. Delightfully fresh and intimate Constable's swiftly painted scenes of windswept landscape recorded the fleeting effects sun and sky.*

ABOVE A Bridge at Borrowdale – *John Constable, 1806. Painted on a sketching tour in Westmorland and Cumberland, this watercolour demonstrates Constable's early talent for design and skill in depicting effects of natural light.*

drawing with the brush as well as the pencil. Throughout his life Constable constantly made studies outdoors, *en plein air*; working directly in watercolour, pen and wash and oil, he would note down the changing effects of weather and time of day. However, many of his larger watercolours were, no doubt, worked-up indoors from his *plein air* sketches.

Constable's drawings are immediate, fresh and intimate. He never composed in a deliberate way, his manner tending rather towards that of swift notation. Yet his compositions remained extremely strong, as he balanced light against shade, mass against void to produce a single, unified whole, Constable's subject was his everyday experience, yet he had the genius to see the extraordinary in the ordinary. As he wrote:

The landscape painter must walk in the fields with a humble mind. No arrogant man was ever permitted to see nature in all her beauty; and, if I may be allowed to use a very solemn quotation, I would say most emphatically to the student, Remember now thy Creator is the days of thy youth!

Constable brought a new freshness to British art.

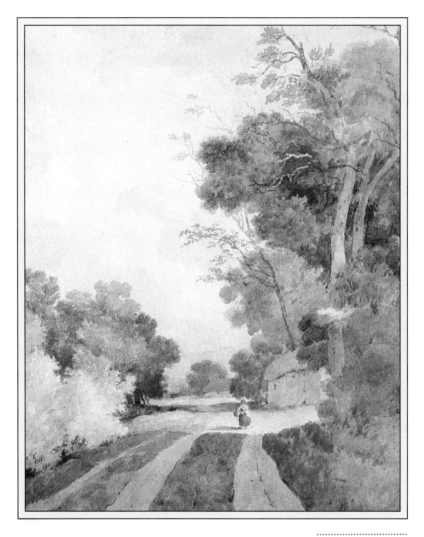

A B O V E Country Lane with Figure – *John Crome. As founder of the Norwich School, he initiated a movement in British landscape painting that advanced the cause of watercolour through the work of John Sell Cotman.*

JOHN CROME AND THE NORWICH SCHOOL

The work of John Crome (1768–1821) was never fully appreciated in his lifetime. He lived quietly and obscurely in Norwich, working as a drawing-master six days a week, with only Sundays left to devote to his own work. In 1803 he founded the Norwich Society, the purpose of which was 'An enquiry into the Rise, Progress and Present state of Painting, Architecture, and Sculpture with a view to point out the Best Methods of study to attain to Greater perfection in these Arts'. The school was composed of 37 artists and held regular exhibitions; Crome alone contributed 27 exhibits to the Society's first exhibition. In 1806 John Sell Cotman joined the Society, and other members included John Thirtle, James Stark, Joseph Stannard and John Middleton. Binyon wrote of the School:

> Norwich was the only place which possessed artists of sufficient strength to create a rival centre to London, and the Norwich School would not have been possible had Crome left his native city for London, like every other genius of the provinces.

Crome's watercolours are rare but distinctive. He used watercolour washes to enchance his work in chalk or pencil. They were usually made for his own purposes, often as preparatory sketches for his oils, and they demonstrate the same pale colours and qualities of spaciousness that his oils contain.

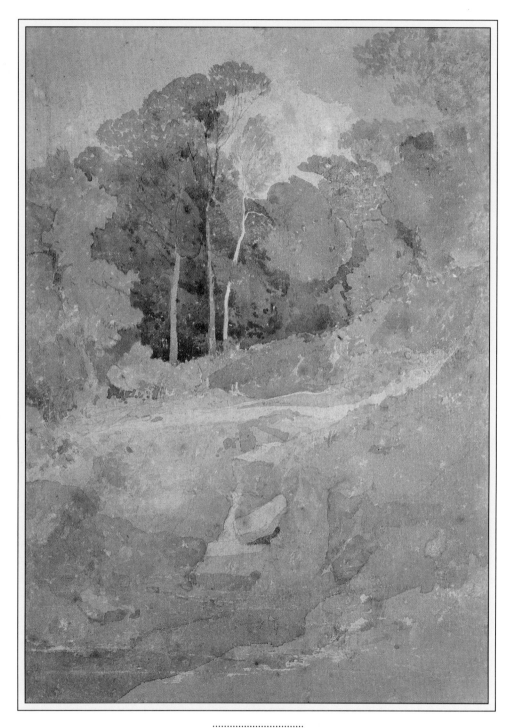

A B O V E Duncombe Park, Yorkshire – *John
Sell Cotman, 1805-6. Balancing one coloured
area against another, Cotman constructed
landscapes from clean, flat washes of
watercolour.*

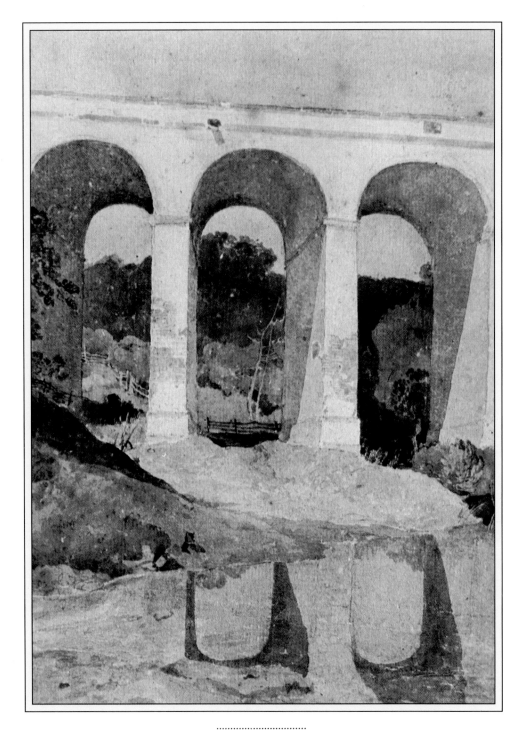

ABOVE Chirk Aqueduct – *John Sell
Cotman, c1806-7. The stark simplicity of theme,
bold composition and crisply applied washes in
this remarkable work combined to make it a
landmark in the evolution of Cotman's style.*

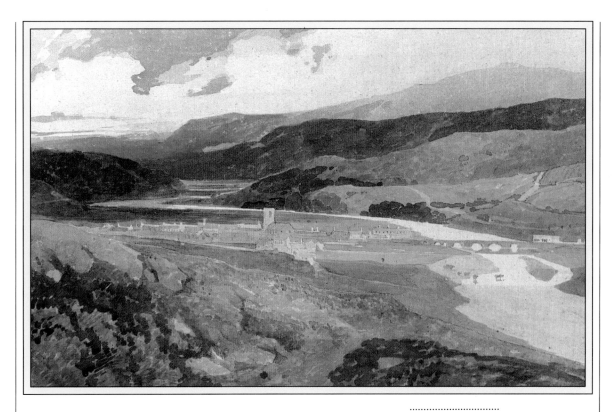

JOHN SELL COTMAN

Cotman (1782–1842) was rather less parochial in his attitude to painting, as a young man he worked at Sir George Beaumont's, alongside Girtin, while the famous Dr Monro was an early patron. He later became president of the society, 'The Brothers', formed originally by Girtin, for the study of romantic landscape. Through the society he came into contact with John Varley, from whom he learnt the technique of laying in clean, flat washes of pure colour.

Cotman went on to incorporate this technique into his own unique style. Working indoors, from pencil notes and outdoor observation, he constructed, with extreme care and deliberation, compositions of stark 'modern' simplicity, such as *Chirk Aqueduct*. This was the first in a series of what can only be described as masterpieces in the art of watercolour: *The Drop Gate at Duncombe Park*, *A Shady Pool*, *Greta Woods* and *Greta Bridge*. The latter is the most famous drawing of this period. It is decidedly not a replica of nature, but rather a reconstruction in paint of the scene Cotman saw before him. Cotman created a pattern of colour, line, tone and mass, perfectly balancing one element against another in a display of masterly control. He

ABOVE Dolgelly, North Wales – *John Sell Cotman. While on a sketching tour of North Wales in 1802, Cotman made outline pencil drawings from which he would later construct the final watercolour in his studio.*

realized the expressive potential of line; every mark is an essential element in the overall design of the work. With hindsight, it is easy to draw striking parallels with the technique of Japanese wood-block printing, and it is largely due to our modern appreciation of such qualities that Cotman's work has undergone such radical reappraisal in the 20th century. As in the Japanese print, shadow is not represented as a negative element in Cotman's work. Rather, he transforms light and dark into simple, interlocking areas of pure colour, in a manner which anticipates the work of such masters as Matisse or Cézanne.

Sadly, Cotman's work was never truly appreciated in his day; he was forced to spend much of his time teaching in order to support his wife and family. The extreme hardships, struggles and disappointments he endured during his lifetime caused Cotman to become morose and despondent. After his death in 1842, a sale of his drawings and paintings raised the paltry sum of £219 17s 6d.

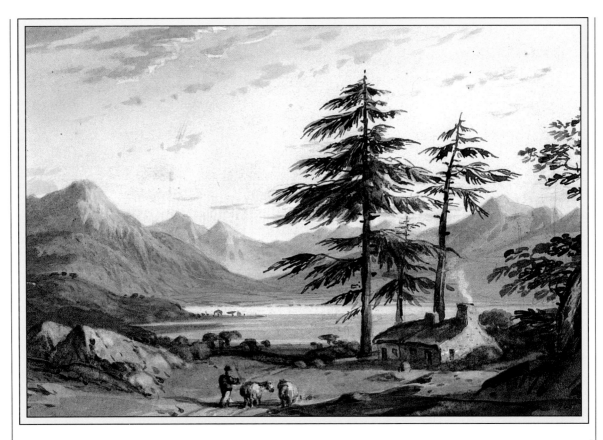

JOHN VARLEY:
MASTER OF THE BROAD WASH

John Varley (1778–1842) was a consummate craftsman and a watercolourist of great skill and influence. One of the most notable of the original members of the Old Water-Colour Society, his influence may be detected in the work of a wide range of his contemporaries, from Linnell, Mulready, Copley Fielding, Cotman and Cox to Samuel Palmer. He was an extraordinary character, unconventional, confident, humorous and combative, and he worked incessantly, continually developing and refining his technique. Varley was schooled in the watercolour tradition of Sandby and Girtin; he was a member of the sketching club founded by Girtin and continued by Cotman. When, in 1804, he became a founder member of the Old Water-Colour Society he was considered to be one of the leading watercolourists in London.

Varley was an enthusiastic teacher, eager to convey his great enthusiasm and the breadth of his technical knowledge to amateurs and professionals alike. Archdeacon Fisher wrote to Constable of Varley's advice: "Principles he says, are the thing. *The warm grey, the cold grey, and the round touch*". Varley would instruct his pupils in the use of flat washes of colour, comparing these to silences, for as every whisper may be distinctly heard in a silence, so every lighter or darker touch on a simple and masterly 'lay-in' told at once. For the benefit of beginners Varley published his *Treatise on the Principles of Landscape Design*.

One of Varley's most extraordinary traits was his sincere belief in astrology; he would immediately request the date and hour of birth of any new acquaintance. He was introduced to William Blake in 1818 and became a constant companion and admirer of Blake's visionary portraits. Technically, Varley's work may be divided into three periods: his early work, influenced by Girtin, consisting of low-toned, thin colour washes: the second phase, when he began to apply the principles of compositional construction he observed in the work of the old masters, Claude and Poussin; and the final period, in which his talent unfortunately became increasingly diluted. As technique replaced any true feeling in his work, he produced classical landscapes flooded with violent colour.

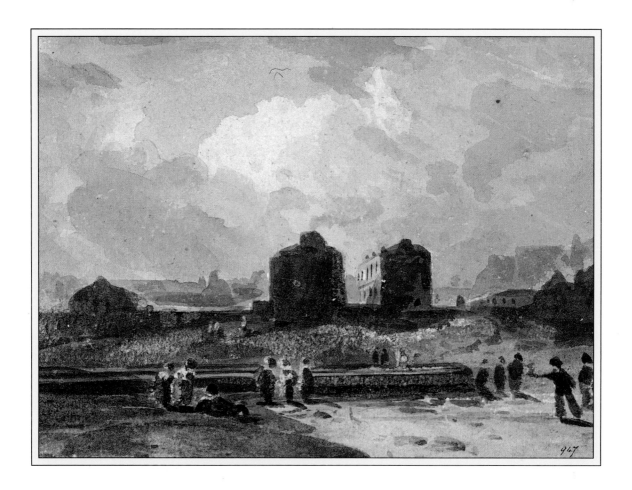

O P P O S I T E **Lake Scene** *– John Varley.*
Through his extensive work as a teacher and
writer on watercolour technique, Varley
contributed greatly to the popularisation of the
art form. An extraordinary character known to
his friends as 'the astrologer', he established many
of the basic ground rules of water painting.

A B O V E **Coast Scene** *– John Varley.*

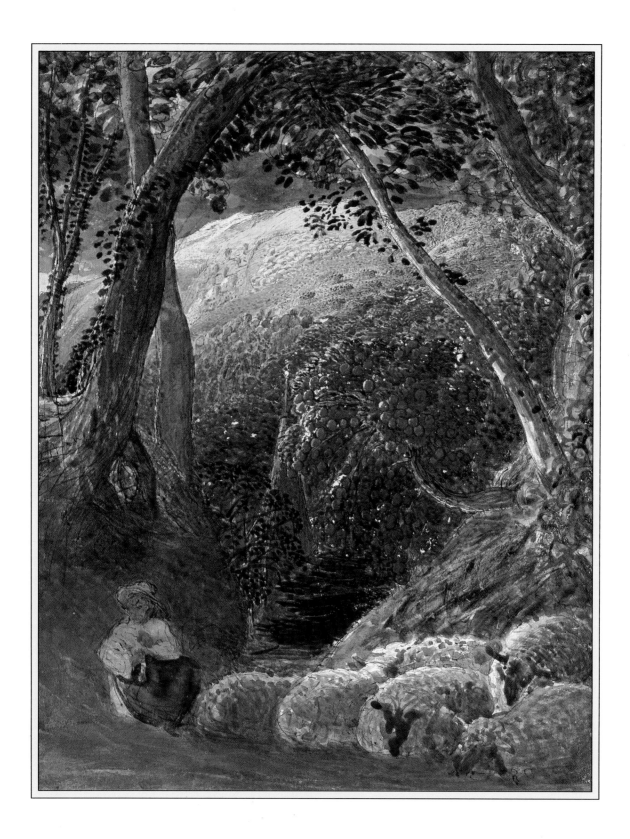

SAMUEL PALMER: THE INWARD EYE AND THE OUTWARD GAZE

The most significant event in the life of the artist Samuel Palmer (1805–1881) was his introduction to William Blake. Varley, John Linnell and Blake met regularly in 1824, and Palmer was introduced to these meetings by Linnell (his future father-in-law), an established artist who had worked with Dr Monro. The 'memory of hours spent in familiar converse' with Blake shaped Palmer's whole approach to his art. In 1825 he wrote in his sketch-book:

> I sat down with Mr. Blake's Thornton's *Virgil* wood-cuts before me . . . They are visions of little dells, and nooks and corners of Paradise; models of the exquisitest pitch of intense poetry . . . Depth, solemnity, and vivid brilliancy only coldly and partially describe them. There is in all such a mystic and dreamy glimmer as penetrates and kindles the inmost soul.

Palmer, painting in the village of Shoreham in Kent which he called his 'valley of vision', produced imaginative landscape drawings in bistre, sepia and Indian ink. Unlike Blake, for whom the visible and the invisible worlds were one, Palmer made constant detailed studies from the countryside around him, and his many sketchbooks bear testament to his skill and observation. However, his drawings were made with the eye of a visionary; in 1824 he wrote:

> I will begin a new sketch-book and, I hope, try to work with a child's simple feeling and with the industry of humility.

Like-minded artists gathered around Palmer in Shoreham, and even Blake visited the village. The group called themselves 'The Ancients', and proceeded to immerse themselves in a romantic vision of the past, searching Virgil's *Eclogues* and Milton's earlier poems for records of primitive life. Their aim was to reconcile creative imagination with a literal, almost scientific representation of nature's appearance, closely anticipating the Pre-Raphaelite Brotherhood of a generation later.

....
OPPOSITE The Magic Apple Tree – *Samuel Palmer. Shoram (in Kent, England) became the inspiration for Samuel Palmer's visionary masterpiece which form a link between the work of Blake and that of the younger generation of Pre-Raphaelite painters.*
....

THE CONNECTION WITH FRANCE RICHARD BONINGTON

In the first half of the 19th century the watercolour medium was rarely used by painters in France, and the great masters of British watercolour were almost unknown. The link with France was finally made when the English watercolourist Richard Bonington (1801–1828) migrated to Calais with his family at the age of 15. Trained by Francia, who had worked with Varley and Girtin, Bonington absorbed the traditions of English watercolour art, particularly the virtue of simplicity in method. He then went to study under Delacroix and Gros in Paris, early demonstrating his skill in producing watercolours full of brilliant light and colour. Working constantly, Bonington made sketching tours of France, Britain and Venice, producing a vast quantity of work before he died in 1828, at the tragically early age of 26. He exhibited two oils and a watercolour (receiving a gold medal) at the highly influential Salon of 1824, which is said to have given new impetus to French painting; it was the starting point of the Barbizon School.

The novel technique of English painters such as Bonington, Copley Fielding and Constable, allowed them to reproduce the sparkling effects of open air in their landscapes. The strength of Bonington's work was its breadth and directness, the great sureness of his work; this was achieved largely through his ability to maintain the brilliant clarity of his first washes of colour. As his work developed, the washes became thinner and more fluid, though he also employed body colour in creating stronger areas of colour. It was his emotional appeal as a colourist which won the admiration of the French; he knew how to combine cold notes of grey with warmer and more positive tones, serene washes with vibrant flicks of colour. He became known for the quality of his brushwork, as he used the point of the brush for deft, flickering strokes and hatchings. Another technical device Bonington utilized was the use of a broken granular wash which, stippled and scumbled with a dry brush, produced an effect of glittering, broken light that was highly effective but never slick or facile. In 1824 he began to apply gum (probably gum arabic) as a varnish, to give depth and translucency to his shadows. The increasing use of bodycolour and varnish may have derived from Bonington's work in oil, in an attempt to achieve equal intensity in the watercolour medium.

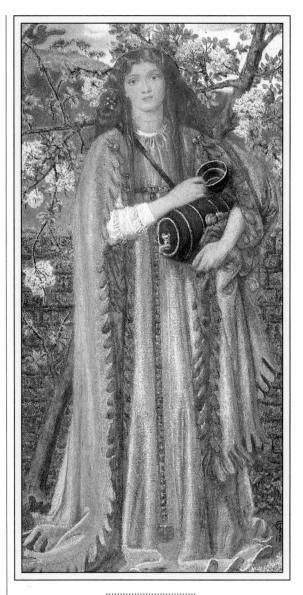

....
A B O V E Golden Water – *Dante Gabriel
Rossetti. Rossetti developed an unorthodox
watercolour technique in order to best convey
characteristic effects of rich ornament and
minutely observed detail.*

....

THE PRE-RAPHAELITES

The Pre-Raphaelite Brotherhood was founded in
London in 1848 by a group of young artists who rejec-
ted the staid and overblown academic establishment
of the time. Seeking a return to a simple, naturalistic
and unaffected approach to art, the Brotherhood
found inspiration in the work of the medieval painters,
before the time of Raphael. The leading figures among
the Pre-Raphaelites were Dante Gabriel Rossetti
(1828–82), William Holman Hunt (1827–1910), Edward
Burne-Jones (1833–98) and John Everett Millais
(1829–96). In their paintings they attempted to recap-
ture the spirit of the medieval world, imitating the
style and subject matter of 14th- and 15th-century art.
Inspired by religious, mythical and romantic legends
(*Mortre d'Arthur* proved a popular source), the Pre-
Raphaelites aimed at transposing fact into fantasy. At
the same time, they demanded absolute and uncompromising truth to nature, rebelling against the more
generalized treatment of form espoused by Reynolds
and his school: thus poetic idealism was fused with
scientific objectivity.

The Pre-Raphaelites worked mainly in oils, but they
also used watercolour and gouache, albeit in a manner
which, at the time, was somewhat unorthodox. Instead
of using transparent washes, they applied the colour
densely, with as little water as possible, so that the
surface of the finished picture resembled that of fresco
or egg tempera, and the intense colours glowed like
stained glass. This technique was well suited to the
Brotherhood's style of painting, which incorporated
rich ornamentation and minutely observed details of
flowers, foliage and fruits.

Some idea of the romantic spirit which imbued the
Pre-Raphaelite movement is conveyed by the comments
of Burne-Jones:

> I mean by a picture, a beautiful romantic dream of
> something that never was, never will be – in a better
> light than any light that ever shone – in a land no
> one can define or remember, only desire – and the
> forms are divinely beautiful.

WATERCOLOUR IN EUROPE

In the early 19th century, lack of suitable paints and
papers had detracted from watercolour's popularity
in continental Europe. In Britain, on the other hand,
manufacturers like James Whatman answered the
demands for special sized and textured papers, just as
men like William Reeves had begun to produce easily
portable cakes of colour in the closing decades of the
previous century. Thus the rapid evolution of watercolour in Britain, and the technical advances that had
accompanied the British school's rise to dominance in
the field, finally began to encourage artists in other
parts of Europe to turn to watercolour, in France in
particular.

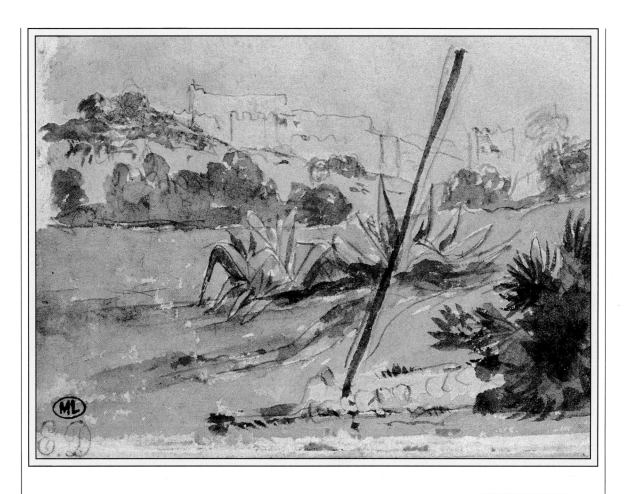

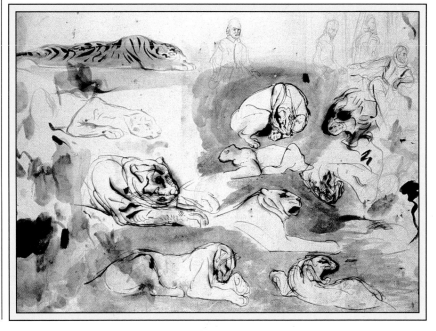

A B O V E Passage du
Maroc avec des Aloes –
*Eugene Delacroix. The
portability of watercolour
enabled Eugene Delacroix to
swiftly record his observations
and impressions while
travelling in North Africa.*

L E F T Sketches for
'Cromwell at Windsor
Castle' – *Eugene Delacroix.
Delicate watercolour washes,
combined with line drawing
in pencil or pen and ink,
proved to be a useful sketching
device for preliminary studies.*

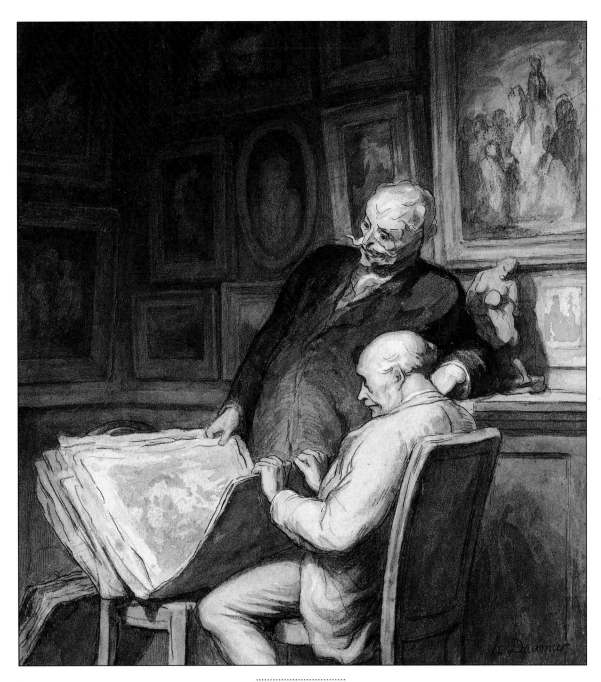

A B O V E **The Print Collectors** – *Honoré Daumier. In France watercolour became a favourite medium for social commentators such as Honoré Daumier, whose watercolour illustrations were reproduced and circulated as lithographic prints.*

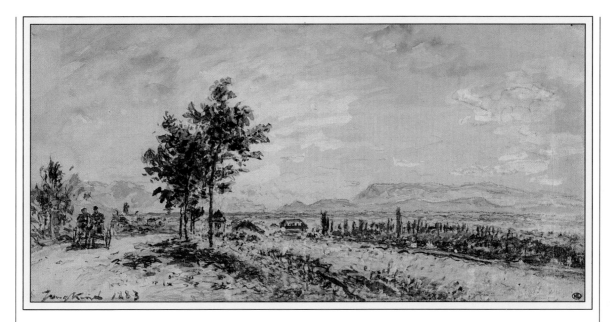

A B O V E Vue de la Côte Saint André –
Johan Barthold Jongkind. Plein-air *artists
quickly recognised the value of watercolour as a
means of recording rapidly shifting effects of
light and atmosphere.*

From 1820 onwards the example of British artists such as Richard Parkes Bonington, Constable and Turner, inspired a whole school of French watercolourists, including such major figures as Eugène Delacroix (1798–1863) and Théodore Géricault (1791–1824). Encouraged by his contact with Bonington, Delacroix became a particularly individual and skilled user of the medium, experimenting with watercolour's fluidity, expressive potential and chromatic brilliance. As British paints and paper were made available to artists elsewhere in Europe, local manufacturers began to compete and by the second half of the century the popularity of watercolour was well established.

In France, watercolour became the favourite medium of the social commentators Eugène Lami, Constantin Guys (1802–1892) and Honoré Daumier (1808–1879), whose watercolour illustrations were reproduced and circulated as prints through the comparatively new medium of lithography. The portability of watercolour suited *plein-air* landscape artists such as Eugène Boudin (1824–1898) and the Dutch painter Johan Barthold Jongkind (1819–1891), whose lively beach scenes and evocative watercolour landscapes anticipated Impressionism. Edouard Manet (1832–1883) and Pierre-Auguste Renoir (1841–1919) also revealed a particular allegiance to the medium. Paul Signac (1863–1935), a disciple of the pointillist painter Georges Seurat (1859–1891), employed the medium regularly and with a directness and spontaneity that was entirely modern.

The British watercolour tradition, with its emphasis on spontaneity and economy of means, was continued by Philip Wilson Steer (1860–1942), working at the turn of the century on watercolours that would not have seemed unfamiliar to an artist of Bonington's generation but stand comparison with work by a contemporary like Signac. Another transitional figure was Hercules B Brabazon (1821–1906), whose bravura technique and boldly conceived compositions placed him among the most progressive artists of his day. A member, like Steer, of the New English Art Club, founded in 1886 as an alternative to the Royal Academy, Brabazon had his first one-man show at the age of 71, encouraged by the resident American portrait painter John Singer Sargent (1856–1925). Brabazon's use of watercolour washes in conjunction with Chinese White, an opaque white pigment, enabled him to maintain the atmospheric effects of the watercolour while giving it a greater solidity. His practice of working in body colour directly on tinted paper was used by Brabazon's great mentor, Turner, and later, most successfully by Whistler. His ability to render colour and the fleeting impression persuaded John Singer Sargent to abandon portraiture and turn to watercolour.

AMERICAN
WATERCOLOUR

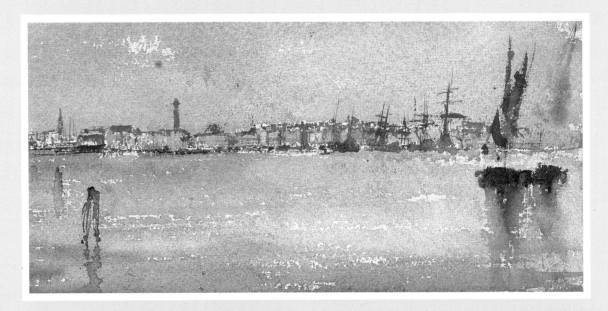

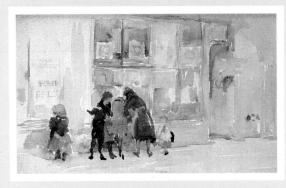

....
TOP Venice Harbour – *James Abbott McNeil Whistler, 1879-80. Whistler achieved the effect of sunlight on water; liquid washes floated on a rough-grained paper, allowing the white paper to sparkle through.*

....
ABOVE Chelsea Children – *James Abbot McNeill Whistler, mid 1880s. Living in Chelsea, Whistler recorded local street life. His use of pure watercolour allows the subject to emerge from the layers of transparent colour.*
....

The history of watercolour in America stretches right back to earliest colonial times. With the exception of the American primitives however, artists in America tended to work in the shadow of their European counterparts, that is until the middle of the 19th century. Continuing cultural ties with Britain made America particularly receptive to watercolour, so much so that in 1866 the American Society of Painters in Watercolour was founded. Many of the artists involved in the rise of American watercolour over this period were also those responsible for the rise of American painting as a whole to international stature. Some, like James Abbott McNeill Whistler (1834–1903) and John Singer Sargent (1856–1925) challenged the Europeans on their own ground, while others, including Thomas Eakins and Winslow Homer, consolidated native American tendencies. Two distinct trends soon became apparent: a realist tradition epitomized by Eakins and Homer, to be continued in the 20th century by artists like Edward Hopper, and the ever-changing tradition of the avant-garde.

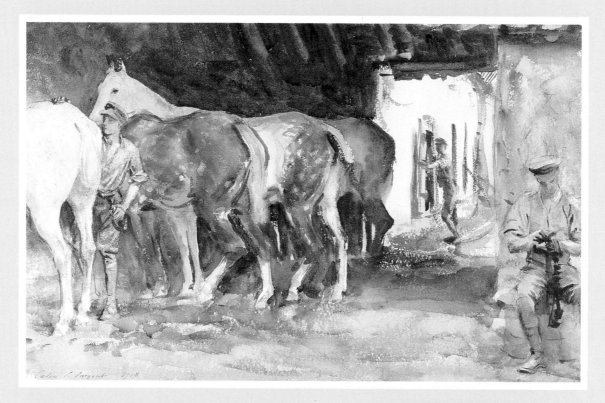

....
A B O V E Scots Greys – *John Singer Sargent.*
The extraordinary facility of John Singer
Sargent's watercolour technique enabled him to
produce an accurate record of life at the front in
a fresh and spontaneous way.
....

James Abbot McNeill Whistler and John Singer Sargent, London-based Americans at a time when Europe welcome a steady stream of artists from the United States, were, without a doubt, two of the most talented expatriate painters of their generation. At the age of 21 Whistler left America, never to return. Having studied in Paris, his contacts with the Parisian art world remained strong long after his decision to settle in London in 1859. His career as a mature water-colourist began around 1880 with an extended stay in Venice. Exploring the city in a gondola converted to a mobile studio, Whistler captured the sparkling effects of the waterways and distant scenes of city architecture with characteristic economy of means. Seascapes and harbour scenes continued to fascinate him. Reducing a scene to its essentials, he applied washes and added summary details with a calligraphic certainty that call to mind Whistler's interest in Japanese art. Responding to a variety of weather conditions, he used evenly spread washes to convey effects of mist, saturated washes casually blotted to produce an illusion of cloud, and washes allowing the surface of the paper to come through to capture effects of sparkling sunlight. A series of watercolour Nocturnes, painted on a visit to Amsterdam, reveal his controlled mastery of the medium in the use of the technique known as 'wet into wet', in which liquid washes are applied to wet paper, or allowed to flow into each other.

John Singer Sargent turned to watercolour around 1990 and quickly became the leading bravura water-colourist of the day. Although he considered himself an American and was indeed a citizen of the United States, Sargent was neither born in America nor ever really lived there. Having spent a cosmopolitan child-hood in Europe, he studied art in Paris and was resident in London for a long period, during which he continued to travel regularly to the Continent and the United States, also visiting Egypt, North Africa and the Middle East. Originally intended as a relief from his portraits in oil, Sargent's watercolours are 'paintings about place' that may or may not contain figures. Employing a close-up viewpoint associated more often with photography, he usually chose to dispense with conventional landscape composition, divided into foreground, background and sky, and opted for a

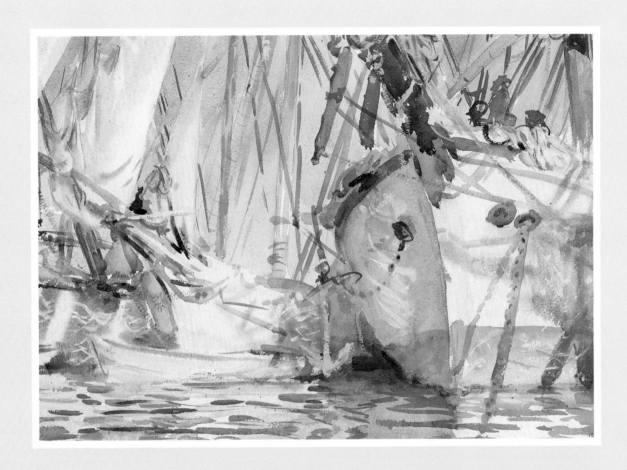

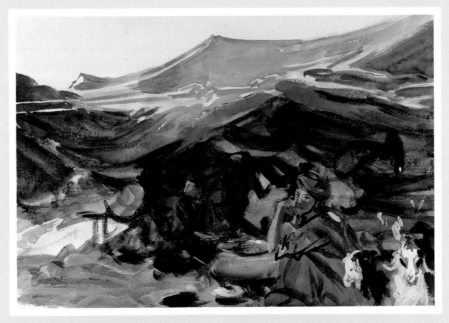

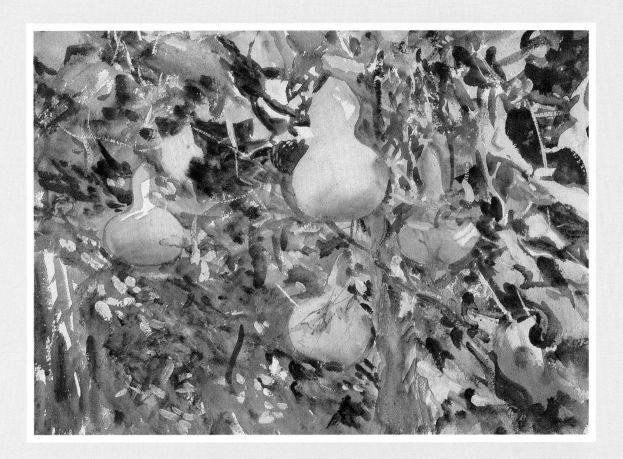

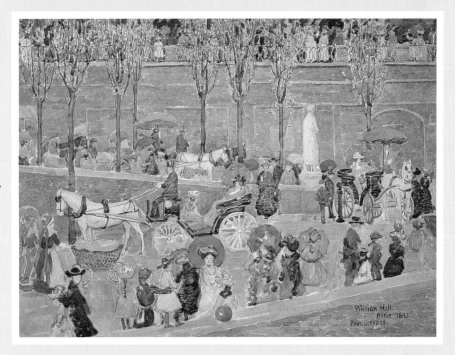

ABOVE Gourds – *John Singer Sargent. Employing a close-up viewpoint, Sargent focused in on his subject, capturing shifting effects of sunlight and shadow in an exciting and unified composition.*

RIGHT Pincian Hill, Rome – *Maurice Prendergast, 1898. Prendergast's tightly designed, brightly coloured, mosaic-like watercolours were a personal response to European impressionism.*

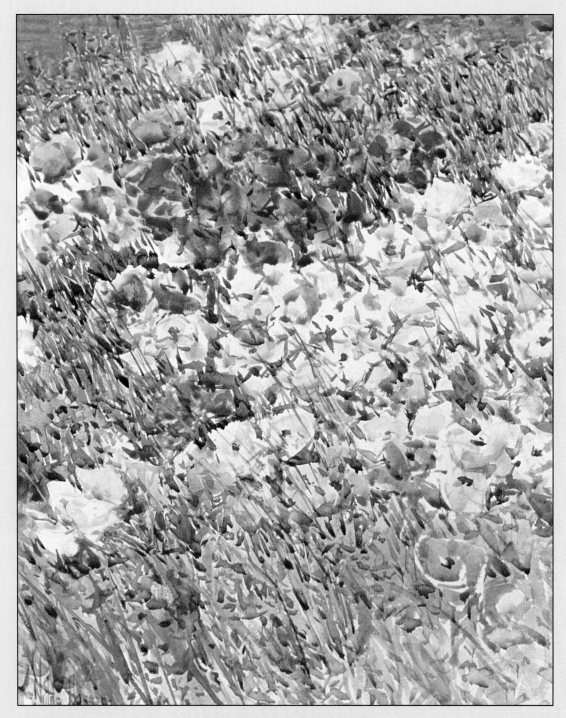

A B O V E The Island Garden – *Childe
Hassam, 1892. Inspired by Claude Monet's
Impressionism, Hassam painted the famous
garden of his friend Celia Thaxter on the island
of Appledore. He captured the flickering effects
of air, sunlight and water.*

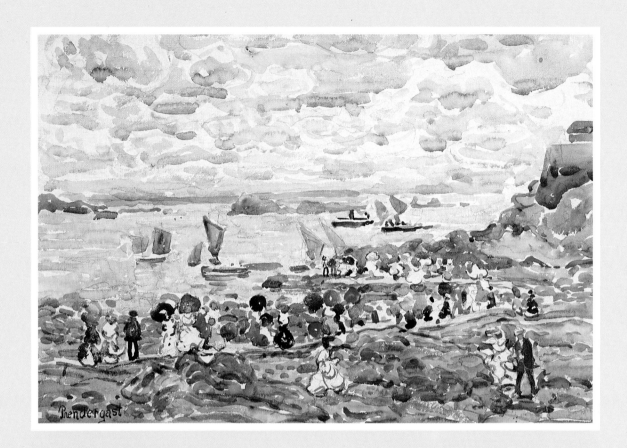

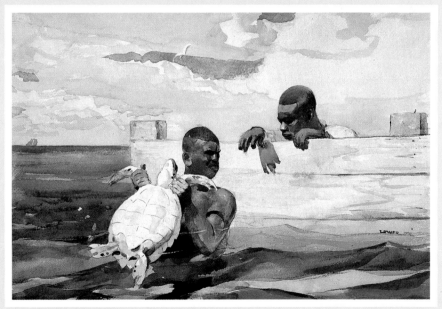

ABOVE St. Malo, No. 1 –
Maurice Prendergast,
c1907–1910. A more fluid
example of Prendergast's
watercolour style, this
unselfconscious rendering of
the beach at St. Malo is a
particularly refreshing
depiction of everyday life.

RIGHT The Turtle Pond
– Winslow Homer, 1898.
The greatest American
watercolourist of his
generation, Winslow Homer
helped foster a tradition of
realism in the United States,
which remained valid long
after it seemed anachronistic
to European modernists.

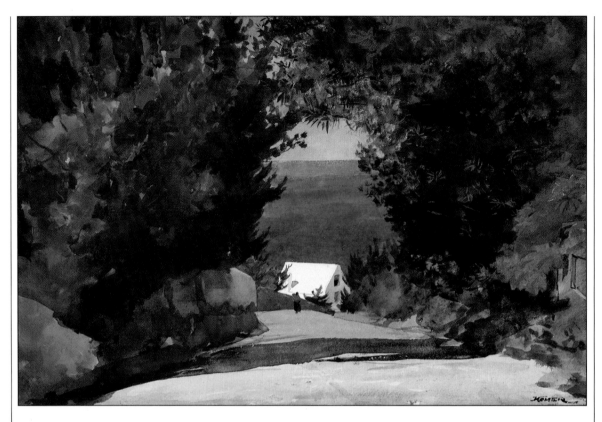

A B O V E Road in Bermuda – *Winslow Homer, 1899–1901. With denses washes of bold watercolour, Homer successfully conveyed the intense atmosphere of sunlight and colour by contrasting light shapes against dark foliage.*

flattened allover composition by focusing in on his subject. Lively, improvisational brushstrokes and overlapping wishes of colour seem to activate the entire picture plane of these closely cropped paintings, in an attempt to capture shifting effects of sunlight and shadow, describe form and surface textures. Always fresh and spontaneous, Sargent's watercolours provide a marvellous record of the artist responding directly to the world around him with unfailing skill and extraordinary facility.

While Whistler was the first American to participate in the new French art emerging in the 1860s, others, like Childe Hassam (1859–1935) and Maurice Prendergast (1858–1924) were important forces in the Americanization of that art. Both men were born in Boston and visited Europe, where they trained in Paris at the Académie Julien. Inspired by Impressionism, and especially the work of Claude Monet (1840–1926), Hassam returned to America to paint landscapes and flower-filled gardens in flickering calligraphic strokes of colour that evoke air and sunlight. Experimenting with a Post-Impressionist mode of painting, Maurice Prendergast soon gained a reputation as one of the more adventurous American painters and in 1908

became one of the founding members of the group in New York known as The Eight. Some of his finest watercolours were painted on a visit to Italy, which inevitably included Venice. His powerful sense of design and systematic use of interlocking patches of colour that derive from the pointillist practice of Paul Signac, combine to produce striking, animated paintings of the crowd-filled squares and busy thoroughfares of Venice. Arriving at this individual interpretation of recent European art, Prendergast showed that it was possible to absorb these influences without fearing loss of identity.

It was as if to protect his native artistic identity that Winslow Homer (1836–1910) developed the matter-of-fact pragmatism that so distinguishes his art. The greatest American watercolourist of his generation, Homer helped forge a tradition of realism that con-

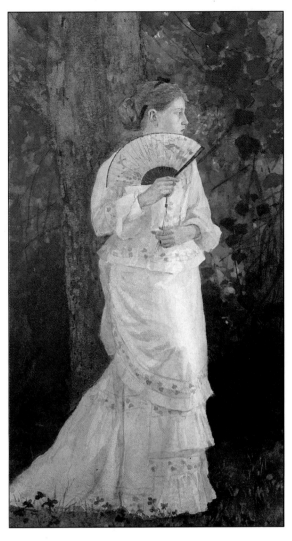

RIGHT The Trysting
Place – *Winslow
Homer, 1875. A typical
example of Homer's early
illustrational work, in this
somewhat contrived
composition watercolour is
used as a convenient
substitute for oil.*

tinued to thrive long after any equivalent activity in advanced European art. Sharing with Thomas Eakins, his contemporary, a belief that the painter should concern himself above all the factual realities of the known world, Homer responded to his American environment in an honest and unbiased way. An illustrator early in his career, he began to paint seriously, first in oil and then in watercolour, in his mid-20s and late 30s. His first powerful works in the watercolour medium were painted around 1881 at the English fishing village of Cullercoats in Tynemouth. On his return to America he settled on the Maine coast, and over the next three decades, on his travels to the Caribbean, New York's Adirondack mountains and Quebec, painted those watercolours which helped launch the independent American watercolour tradition.

Fine examples of classic watercolour technique derived from British practices, Homer's paintings also embody a robustness and a candid, 'snap shot' effect that is entirely American. The wilderness scenes from his hunting expeditions in the mountains are an unsentimental celebration of humanity's struggle against the wild forces of nature. Far from heroic, the hunters and guides in these pictures are treated as rather anonymous figures, concerned only with their day-to-day survival. The strong light and vibrant colours in the Bahamas and Bermuda presented Homer with an exciting new challenge. Using dense washes of bold colour, he successfully conveyed the intensity of the heat and by contrasting light shapes against darker accents, indicated the brightness of the sunlight with breathtaking results.

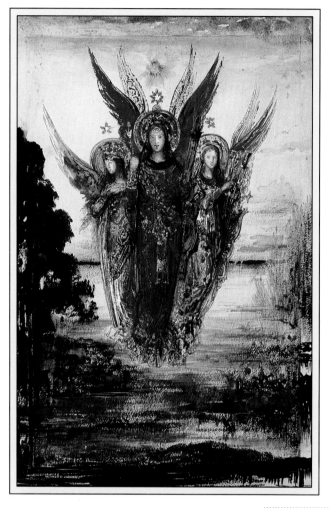

A B O V E Voix du Soir – *Gustave Moreau.*
Gustave Moreau's extremely bold handling of the
watercolour medium, his use of jewel-like colour,
floated in translucent washes onto a rough
grained paper was highly influential on later
generations of painters.

EUROPEAN WATERCOLOUR ART
AT THE TURN OF THE CENTURY

At the turn of the century, young artists in Continental Europe were involved in activities very different to those that preoccupied their American contemporaries. The visionary outlook of Symbolist writers and artists provoked imaginative experiments, seen at their most exciting in the watercolour work of Gustave Moreau (1828–98) and Odilon Redon (1840–1916). They exploited the richness of colour to be found in transparent watercolour washes, and the luminosity of the medium was carried over into their oil and pastel works.

In numerous compositional studies and sketches for his ambitious mythological subjects in oil, Gustave Moreau used watercolour in an unusually bold way for an artist of his generation. Floating colour on to rough paper, sometimes combining it with pastel or pen and ink, and allowing the white paper to show through, Moreau created shimmering surfaces of jewel-like intensity, more animated than anything he was to produce in oil. Seemingly random patches of pigment are brushed or spattered over loosely applied areas of wash, made opaque in some passages to provide a pastel-like appearance. As a watercolourist, Moreau was one of the most inventive artists of the late 19th century and the extraordinary breadth of handling in these works, some of which are tiny, anticipate the methods of later 20th century painters.

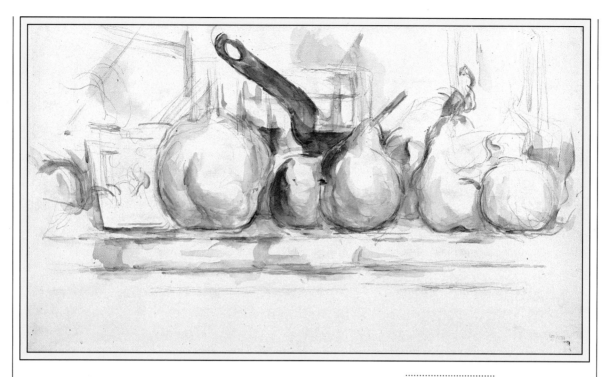

CÉZANNE: THE FATHER OF MODERN PAINTING

The two artists who contributed most to a modern approach to watercolour were Paul Cézanne (1839–1906) and Auguste Rodin (1840–1917). Known chiefly for their work in other media, both were also highly skilled watercolourists.

Although Cézanne was loosely associated with the Impressionists, he was sceptical of much of their work. He believed the truth of nature lay far deeper than in surface effects; he was not concerned with copying the landscape but in recognizing the elemental forces behind nature. What appealed to him were nature's solidity and permanence. He extracted colour and form and modelled them with planes of pure colour, composing his paintings into a tightly interwoven structure. The painter Emile Bernard describes Cézanne's technique:

> He began on the shadow with a single patch of colour, which he then overlapped with a second, then a third, until all these tints, forming successive screens, not only coloured the object but modelled its form.

Towards the end of his life, Cézanne achieved a masterly control over the watercolour medium. Attempting to record – tentatively at first, then with increasing confidence – the mass of visual material that met his eye, he applied dabs of colour and hatched pencil marks that activated the white paper and succeeded in bringing the entire image to life. Cézanne realized that the white of the paper support, left bare in parts to represent light, also served to represent space. At the same time, this expansive use of the paper support emphasizes the picture plane, and the image becomes easy to read as a series of colours and marks on a flat surface. Even though it was this last aspect of his work that proved so intriguing to later artists, notably the Cubists, Cézanne was concerned to define space and volume rather than dissolve it. Colour modulations culled from Impressionist practices were Cézanne's primary means of modelling form, and he used the advancing and receding properties of warm and cool colours to model the advancing and receding planes of his subject. In the late watercolours, colours describe form and seem to dissolve it – another paradox that made his work so fascinating. Cézanne gave the world a new way of seeing, and thus is frequently called the father of modern art.

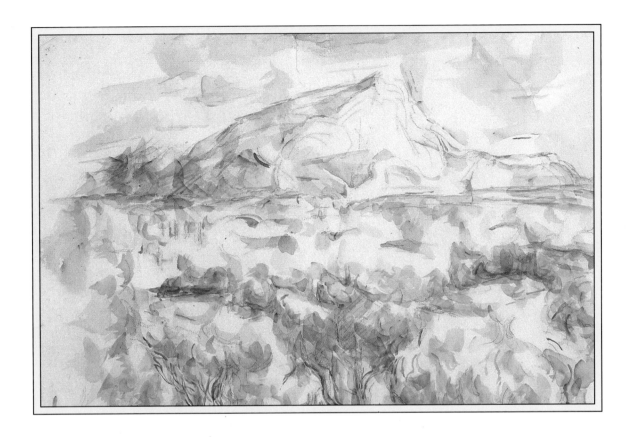

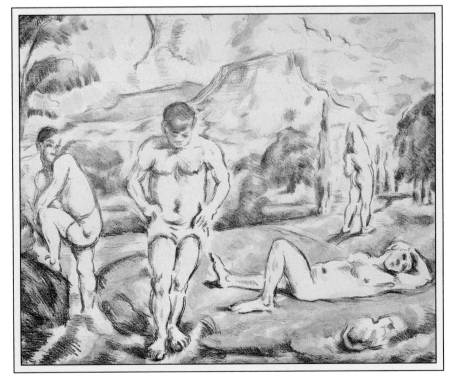

ABOVE **Montagne Sainte Victoire** – *Paul Cézanne. Mount Sainte Victoire, Cézanne's most famous landscape motif, is seen in the distance, a shimmering, mirage-like image, floating before our eyes. Here, Cézanne makes extensive use of the untouched white surface of the paper in order both to construct and dissolve the form of the mountain.*

LEFT **The Bathers** – *Paul Cézanne.*

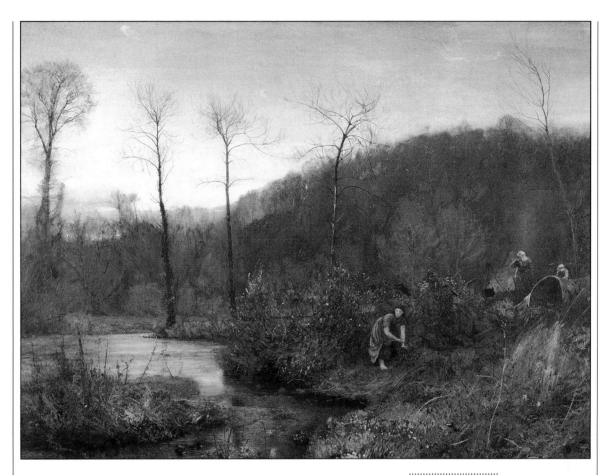

A B O V E **A Gipsy Encampment** – *John William North. JW North, a trained wood engraver, achieved fame with his atmospheric and highly evocative landscapes.*

At the same time that Cézanne's watercolours were beginning to exert an influence, Auguste Rodin's were similarly attracting attention when they were exhibited in Paris and New York. Whereas Cézanne treated watercolour as a branch of painting, Rodin used it primarily as an extension to drawing. His remarkable, spare wash drawings, begun in the 1890s – generally of the female figure, clothed or unclothed, and often in attitudes relating to dance – created quite a stir when first exhibited. Deceived by their apparent simplicity, many critics dismissed them while others were offended by the infomality of the poses, made all the more shocking by the way Rodin isolated his figures on a page rather than placing them in a setting. Rodin was a brilliant draughtsman, and the economy of line, directness of statement and powerful sense of design in these late watercolour works ensured his position as a precursor to 20th-century artists, ranging from Henri Matisse to Gustav Klimt, Egon Schiele, and Americans like Charles Demuth. It was through the seemingly innocent medium of watercolour

therefore, that established ways of seeing were already being undermined, opening up possibilities for a younger generation to explore.

DRAUGHTSMEN AND ILLUSTRATORS

During the second half of the 19th century, the increasing popularity of illustrated magazines such as *Once a Week*, *Good Words* and *Cornhill Magazine* encouraged the rise of a group of watercolour painters and illustrators whose work was narrative in content, expressing sentiments highly popular in their day. The revival of English book illustrations was due in large part to the black-and-white work of the Dalziel brothers in the 1860s. The Dalziels ran their own printing and

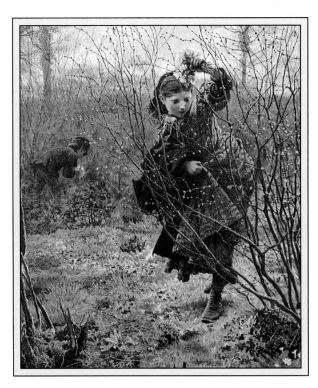

publishing firm and encouraged young artists to produce original drawings for reproduction by the wood-engraver. Rossetti, Millais, Walker, Pinwell and North all produced designs for the wood-block, although they later abandoned it for the freedom of their own original watercolours.

Fred Walker (1840–75) was elected to the Old Water-Colour Society as an associate in 1864, where he exhibited *Spring*, a work typical of his style, in which he skilfully reproduces the natural scene. John William North (1842–1924) was trained as a wood-engraver, becoming a member of the New Water-Colour Society in 1854. He worked for the Dalziels and became best known for his interpretations of landscape in publications such as *Wayside Posies*. His landscape watercolours similarly reveal an almost scientific depiction of detail and his interest in atmosphere and light anticipated that of the French Impressionists. The work of John Pinwell (1842–75) and Arthur Boyd Houghton demonstrates a heightened sensitivity to line, coupled with great inventive and interpretative power. Boyd Houghton made his name with his dramatic illustrations to the Dalziels' *Arabian Nights* (1865).

The 19th century was the golden age of British illustration, when such luminaries as Walter Crane, Kate Greenaway (1846–1901) and Randolph Caldecott (1846–1886) each contributed their own unique style of book illustration. They worked in watercolour, but always took full consideration of the method by which their illustrations were to be reproduced. The process of printing in colour from wood-blocks was revived by the printing entrepreneur Edmund Evans, who printed his own colour children's books from 1877 and commissioned and produced the work of leading illustrators. Of necessity, illustrators worked with pure colours and flat tones, using a simple and direct treatment adapted to the limited scope of the engraver. The most important element in Crane's work is decoration; in his illustrations for *The Song of Sixpence* (1869) *The Baby's Opera* (1877) and *The Floral Fantasy* (1899), both graphic skills and purity of line and colour are imaginatively utilized towards decorative ends, and he took great pains to ensure that pictures and text worked harmoniously together.

Kate Greenaway's delicate watercolours captured an enchanted Regency world which lent itself brilliantly to children's book illustration. She won immediate success with *Under the Window*, which she both wrote and illustrated; 100,000 copies were issued, plus editions in French and German. Caldecott was more of a caricaturist, but in a poetic and romantic vein. He was a master of the economic statement.

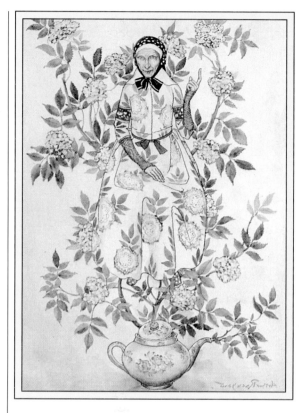

....
A B O V E 'In the midst of the tree sat a
kindly looking old woman' *from* Elder Tree
Mother *by HC Anderson – Arthur Rackham.
Arthur Rackham's extraordinary illustrations
often combine natural and human forms.*
....

ARTHUR RACKHAM

As the century progressed, major advances in mechanical methods of photographic reproduction brought
about a revolution in printing and the three-colour
process took over from all previous methods of colour
reproduction. By the last decade of the 19th century
it was possible for any picture, no matter how varied
and graduated in tint and tone, to be printed by means
of the half-tone process; watercolour drawings could
be reproduced almost in facsimile, rapidly and at comparatively small cost. As a consequence, colour books,
in which the pictorial plate was the central feature,
became widely available and extremely popular. One
of the first artists to cultivate this field was Arthur
Rackham (1867–1939). His colour illustrations to *A
Midsummer Night's Dream* (1908) and *Grimm's Fairy Tales*
(1909) reveal his rich imagination, and the quality of his
use of line and tone. Rackham developed a technique

whereby he would start with a drawing in black and
white, washing on a strong tint of raw umber, which
gave a general tone of warmth to the picture. He would
then, where required, lift the tone with a wet brush and
add notes of pure colour, all the while carefully grading
the tone of the whole. The result was reproduced in
four printings, one for black areas and the others for
the three primary colours.

THE SCOTTISH CONNECTION

William McTaggart's ability as a watercolourist was
unique. His use of high-pitched colour and the
immediacy of his brushwork allowed him to convey
the movement and variation of light and weather in a
manner analogous to that of his contemporaries
abroad, the French Impressionists. Painting out of
doors, *'sur le motif'*, enabled McTaggart to create an
immediate record of his emotional response to nature.
Working on thick, rough-surfaced Whatman paper,
on a scale which allowed his brush to sweep from one
end of the paper to the other, McTaggart would lay
on fresh washes of colour, modulating colour and tone
while the paper was still wet. Sir James Caw wrote of
McTaggart:

> (In watercolour) he began to liberate his hand to
> express the sparkle and flicker of light, the purity
> and brilliance of colour, and the dancing and
> rhythmical motion.

Arthur Melville was another artist concerned to
convey the sparkle of atmosphere and the drama of
movement in his work. However, his technique and
choice of subject matter were very different to those
of McTaggart. Melville worked largely in the East,
notably Turkey, Morocco, the Persian Gulf, Baghdad
and Spain. Technically he developed a method of building up blots, blobs and dashes of pure colour, which
from a distance resolved themselves into a Moorish
procession or an excited crowd of spectators awaiting
a Spanish bullfight. Colour was applied to specially-
prepared paper which had been soaked in diluted
Chinese white; Melville worked on to a wet surface,
running one colour into another.

Of all the Scottish artists, Joseph Crawhall's work
stands out as the most distinctive in its use of pattern,
refinement of tone and swift, economic brushwork.
Animals were his favourite subject, and he often
worked from memory, in the tradition of the Chinese
masters, evoking in a few swift, calligraphic lines the
form of a bull ready to charge, for example.

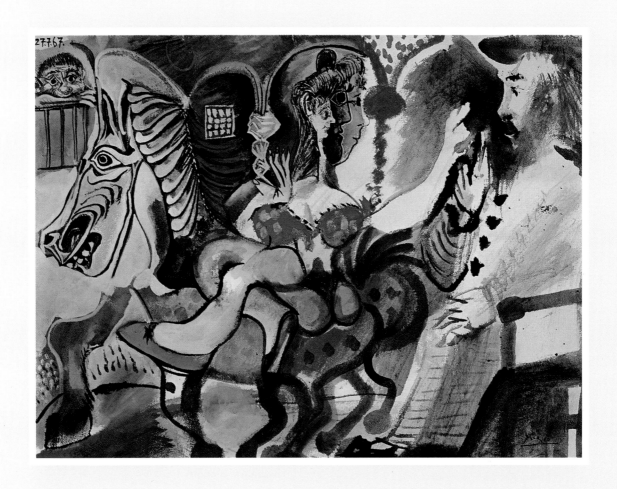

THE 20th CENTURY

he evolution of watercolour in the 20th century has been rapid and experimental. While continuing to flourish in the traditional vein, as a specialist art form with its own societies and devotees, watercolour has also played a significant role in the mainstream developments of modern art. For some major contributers to modernism, such as Pablo Picasso, watercolour formed an integral part of an overall experimental approach; for others, such as Paul Klee, its continued use enabled a subtle exploration of abstract form. Whether employed in transparent washes or combined with other media, watercolour contributed to an investigative approach that was essential to avant-garde activity. The traditional purist definition of watercolour, formulated in the 18th and 19th centuries, has therefore been extended in the 20th century to include watercolour combined with crayon, collage and gouache.

THE FAUVES
WATERCOLOUR

Fauvism exploded onto the art world in 1905, the first of many 'isms' that were to leave their indelible mark on the 20th century. The 1905 Salon d'Automne exhibition of works by Henri Matisse (1859–1954) Maurice de Vlaminck (1876–1958), André Derain (1880–1954) and their followers caused a sensation, with landscapes featuring vivid orange skies, purple water and bright red trees. The art critic Louis Vauxcelles gave the group its name when he pointed to a Donatello-type bust of a child in the same exhibition and described it as being *"au milieu des fauves"* – "in the midst of wild beasts".

The intention of the Fauves was to use colour "like sticks of dynamite", to express the joy of life. Although the subject matter remained figurative, brushwork and colour were freed from the constraints of naturalistic representation.

While most of the Fauves preferred to work in oils, Georges Rouault (1871–1958) took up watercolour and gouache enthusiastically. Excepting his refined sensibility for colour and design however, Rouault's interests had little in common with the more decorative concerns of his colleagues. His watercolours dating from 1905 and 1906, of strolling players, actors, prostitutes and clowns – the outcasts of society – represent an intensely religious attitude towards the tragedy of life that was later expressed through more specifically religious imagery. Ambitious in scale and subject,

these watercolours remain powerful statements in art even today.

In Rouault's later works, heavy blue-black outlines enclosing areas of brightly coloured pigment give the effect of stained glass, recalling Rouault's early apprenticeship in that medium. More gouaches than watercolours, they marked a move away from the transparency of his earlier watercolour technique towards an exciting mixed-media method which imitated the impasto style of his oils.

Raoul Dufy (1877–1953) was a member of the Fauve group from 1906–1908, but eventually developed his own style of landscape and still-life painting. Dufy was particularly fond of watercolours, whose rapid and free-flowing qualities corresponded with the spontaneity of his own vision and style. Indeed, he proved to be one of the few artists at the time to recognize watercolour's potential, both as a sketching tool and as a means of achieving the saturated colour so fundamental to Fauvist experimentation. He wrote:

Watercolour has perhaps the greatest potential for free improvisation. It is scarcely material as a medium, and it is rapid, for the passages between colours are already formed by the white of the paper. It is very pleasant for quick sketches from nature and useful for constructing the basic outlines of a composition. It is above all an art of intentions.

Dufy's passion for Persian art and the wood engravings of Gauguin are evident in works of remarkable vitality, in which he superimposed eloquent, calligraphic line work over areas of brilliant, Fauvist colour. In his long career, Dufy produced 2,000 paintings and countless designs – for the stage, murals, ceramics and textiles – in watercolour. His paintings of the French Riviera – racing scenes, regattas and palm-fringed promenades – have a verve and gaiety which struck a chord with post-war 1920s society, and his influence in the fields of painting, graphics and textile design is still felt today.

Although André Dunoyer de Segonzac (1884–1974) never adhered to any particular movement, his style was firmly rooted in the experiments carried out in Paris during the early years of the century. A skilled etcher and painter in both oil and watercolour, Segonzac was particularly adept at exploiting the watercolour medium. Combining loose pencil drawing with boldly applied colour, his still lifes and landscapes have a freshness and spontaneity often missing in the more ambitious mythological themes and impasto

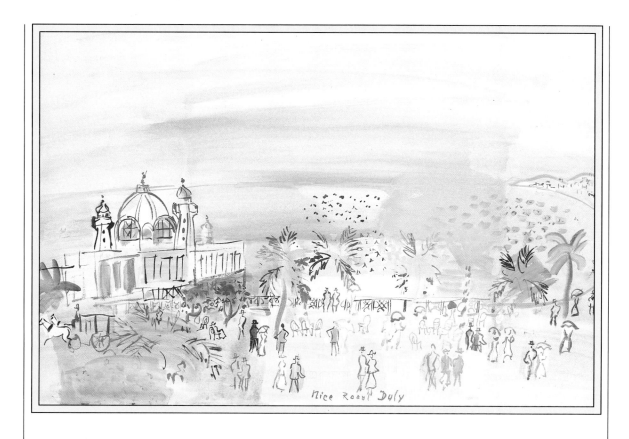

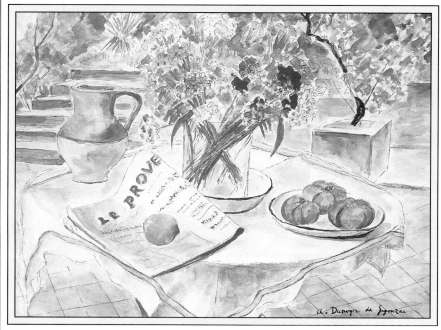

A B O V E Nice, Le Casino –
Raoul Dufy, 1936.
*Combining fluid washes of
saturated colour with
animated brush drawing,
Raoul Dufy's spontaneous
watercolours struck a chord
with post-war society in scenes
of the palm-fringed
promenades of the French
Riviera.*

L E F T Nature Morte au
Provençal – *André Dunoyer
de Segonzac. Dunoyer de
Segonzac's lively watercolours
of still life or landscape scenes
represent the high standard of
work among lesser-known
French artists since Fauvism.*

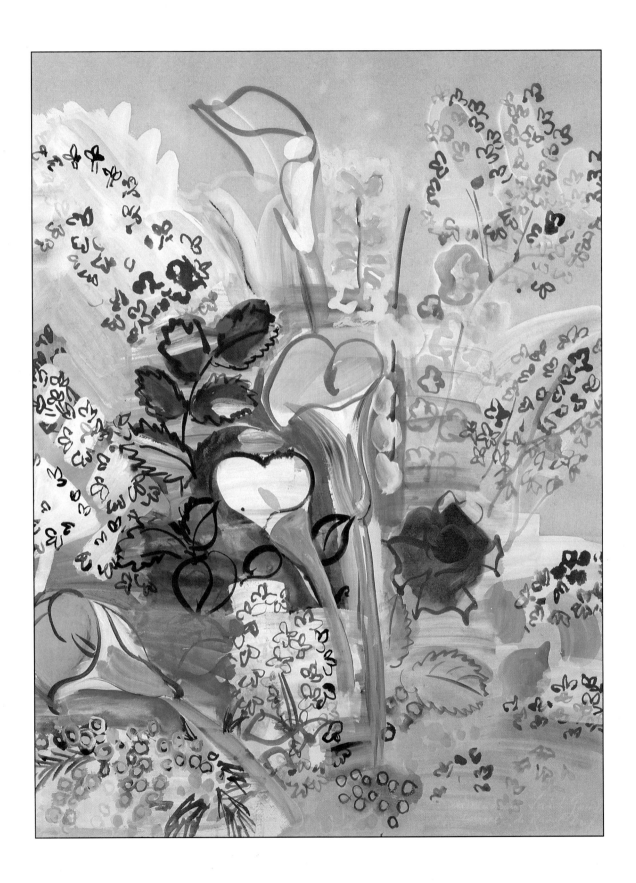

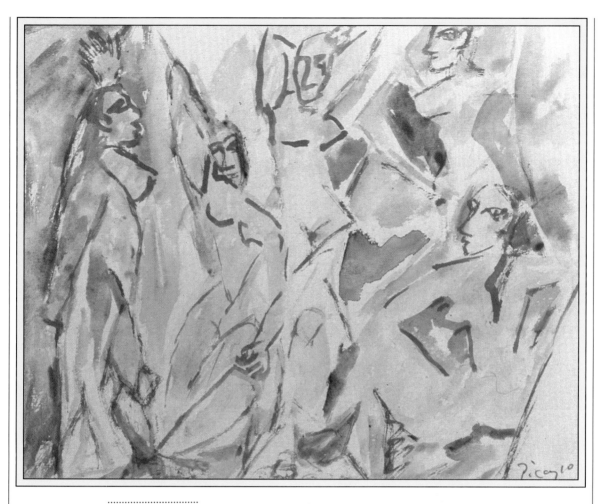

A B O V E Study for Les Demoiselles
d'Avignon *– Pablo Picasso, 1907. Of the many
studies for* Les Demoiselles, *this watercolour
most closely resembles the final composition. The
thinly brushed rough-edged patches of colour in
the oil originate in Picasso's use of watercolour in
studies of this kind.*

L E F T Le Bouquet d'Arums *– Raoul
Dufy, c1939–40. Dufy's exuberant flower study
reveals watercolour's potential as a bold and
colourful sketching medium.*

technique of his oils. Although he failed to win the
recognition that some of his contemporaries won,
Segonzac was nevertheless an extremely talented artist
whose contribution to watercolour painting must not
be overlooked.

Dividing his time between Britain and France, the
English artist Matthew Smith (1879–1959) evolved a
similarly vibrant style through his contact with the
Parisian art world. During the first half of the century
he produced a fine body of work in oil and watercolour
which, in its ease of handling, command of form and
sumptuous colour, was more French than English. In
his landscapes, still lifes, portraits and studies of the
nude, Smith learnt to liberate and intensify his painting through an exuberant use of colour. The bold
linear rhythms and direct, spontaneous brushwork of
his late watercolour still lifes convey the remarkable
fluidity of his mature style.

PICASSO AND CUBISM

The most versatile of 20th-century artists, Pablo
Picasso (1881–1973) frequently employed watercolour
as an experimental tool, his unorthodox technique
ranging from pure transparent watercolour to watercolour combined with body colour, sometimes high-
lighted with chalk or pastel. Living at the Bateau-
Lavoir studios in Monmartre, he became an intimate

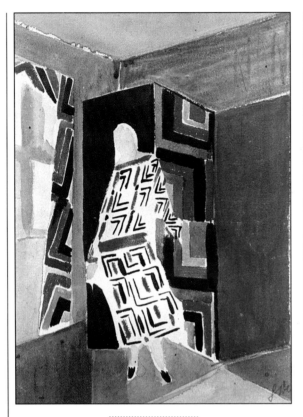

ABOVE Woman – *Sonia Delaunay, 1925.*
Sonia Delaunay developed Robert Delauney's
theories of colour 'simultaneity' in designs for
textiles and tapestries, as well as in her own
paintings.

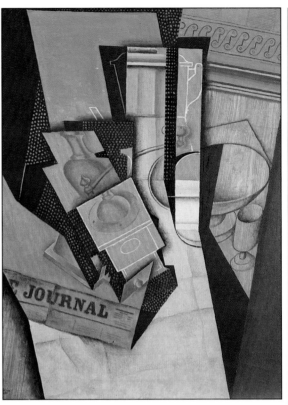

ABOVE Le Petit Déjeuner – *Juan Gris,*
1910–15. Only rarely choosing to work in water
based media, Cubists like Gris frequently
imitated effects of collage in highly patterned,
decorative still lifes of this type.

of symbolist writers and poets such as Max Jacob, André Salmon and Guillaume Apollinaire. His depiction of *saltimbanques* (trapeze artists), known to him through frequent visits to the Cirque Medrano, reveal a link with French literary symbolism and the circus imagery which permeates the poetry of Appollinaire and Jules Laforgue. By 1907, however, when he began work on the canvas that would become known as *Les Demoiselles d'Avignon*, Picasso had embraced a new range of influences, excited by the primitive representation of form in Egyptian and pre-Roman Iberian sculpture, the expressive power of African carvings and masks and the planar fragmentation in Cézanne's watercolours.

This initial experimental work heralded a new era in the history of art. During the next decade, Picasso, Georges Braque (1882–1963) and Juan Gris (1887–1927) took up where Cézanne had left off, rejecting the surface representation of reality that had dominated Western art since the Renaissance and searching instead for the underlying truth, the essence, of the objects they depicted.

Whereas opaque colour had played a dominant role in the early 'blue' and 'pink' periods of Picasso's work, in the many studies for *Les Demoiselles*, Picasso followed Cézanne's lead and capitalized on the transparency of the medium. *Standing Nude* (1908) and a related study are two such works. With her head tilted, elbows thrown up and arms wrapped behind her, the nude is fiercely abstracted in a manner resembling African carving, the various components of her body defined by coloured geometric planes which also serve to indicate volume and space. The fractured forms and thinly applied colour in the study are reflected in the final oil painting.

The radical fragmentation that came to characterize Cubism eventually culminated in the art of collage, or *papier collé*, in which the 'analytical' break-

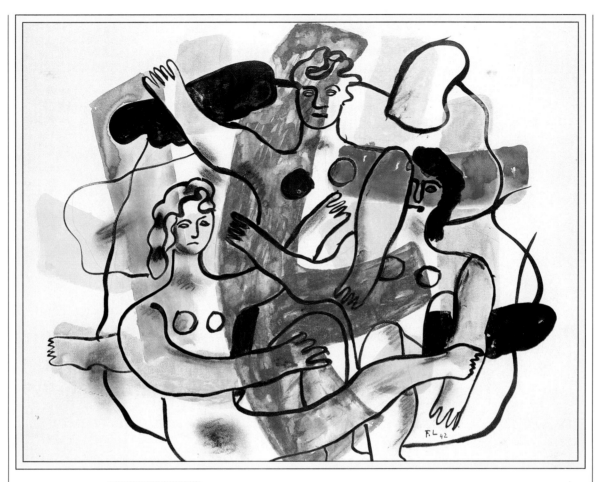

down of objects was succeeded by their 'synthetic' reconstruction. In notebook studies from this period Picasso used watercolour as a sketching medium to record the spatial experiments which preoccupied him at the time. Occasionally combined with crayon drawing, watercolour provided a simple way of suggesting the flat shapes and patterned areas later replaced by collaged elements in the final works.

The lack of conventional modelling in Picasso's Cubist work emphasizes the flatness and patterning that became an essential part of later Cubism. Fernand Léger (1881–1955), in contrast, developed a curvilinear Cubism dependent on dynamic mechanical imagery and robotic figures composed of modelled cones, spheres, cubes and cylinders. Like Picasso, Léger used watercolour as an exploratory medium to complement his work in oils. Abstracted landscapes of trench warfare, painted during his time at the Front, are particularly fine examples of his watercolour work, as are a series of small watercolour still lifes painted later in his career.

Robert Delaunay (1885–1941), the originator of a style called Orphic Cubism, sought to record the dynamics of modern life through pure colour and celebrated a suitably modern subject – the first flight across the English Channel – in his watercolour, *Homage to Bleriot* (1914). Referring to recent scientific texts on the properties of colour, Delaunay believed it possible to create effects of recession and movement in space solely through contrasts of colour. In this particularly lucid example of Delaunay's distinctive brand of Cubism, coloured discs fly through the air, evoking wind currents and flickering sunlight, and the Eiffel tower appears in the distance.

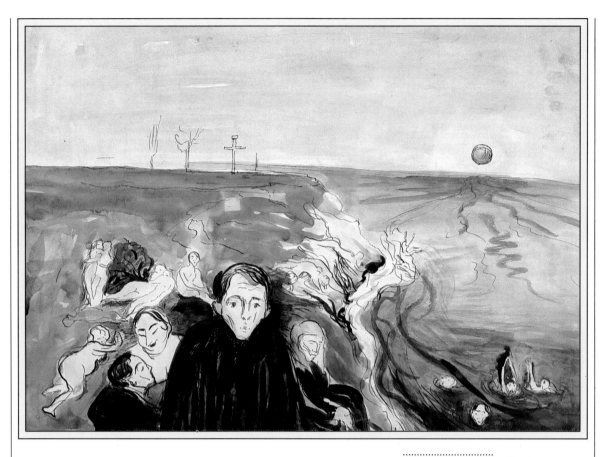

·······························
A B O V E The Empty Cross – *Edvard*
Munch, 1889–1901. A set of work on the theme
of the cross relate closely in style to The Scream,
an example of his highly charged early work.
·······························

Picasso aside, the Cubists did not contribute significantly to the evolution of watercolour. Having learnt from Cézanne how reality can be deconstructed, leading Cubists such as Georges Braque and Juan Gris preferred to work in oils, combining them with sand for greater substance, or in collage, incorporating imitation wood veneer, chair caning or newspaper cuttings into their work. However, among the artists influenced by Cubism, who carried forward aspects of its program without being directly involved in the movement, many – like Macke, Klee and George Grosz – were to become significant watercolourists.

EXPRESSIONISM

Since the closing decades of the 19th century, the chief motivating force behind much avant-garde European art had been the desire to transcend realism. Van Gogh, Gauguin, Redon and the Symbolists had all employed colour, pattern, line and texture for expressive, rather than merely descriptive, purposes: that these elements could convey inner feelings and emo-

tions was particularly intriguing. For artists like van Gogh, the expression of psychological states quickly became self expression, and it was this phenomenon which, in the 20th century, came to be known as Expressionism.

Though not a prolific watercolourist, the Norwegian artist Edvard Munch (1863–1944) was certainly proficient in the medium. A quintessential Expressionist, his work is intensely subjective and psychologically complex. Like van Gogh, Munch suffered from mental illness, and his paintings were highly emotional personal statements on the loneliness and alienation of man. In a particularly emotive series of works dating from the same period in which his famous oil *The Scream* (1893) was painted, watercolour – occasionally combined with pen and ink – provided him with a very direct way of setting down his thoughts

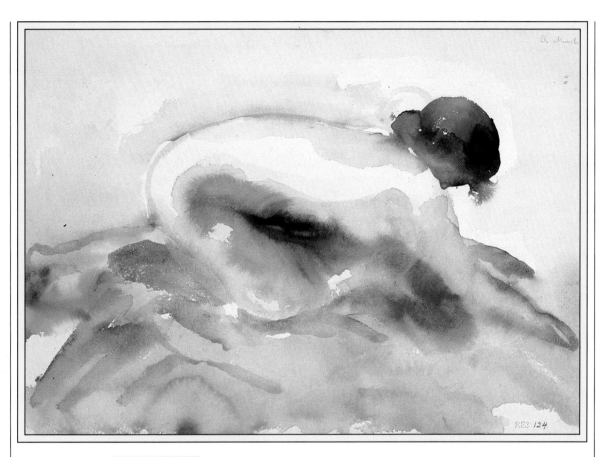

ABOVE Kneeling Nude – *Edvard Munch, 1921. The marvellous fluidity of Munch's later watercolours set in motion a style that came to characterize the watercolour work of Expressionists like Nolde and Kokoshka.*

and emotions. Later figure studies and sketches, from the 1920s, reveal the facility and economy of Munch's mature watercolour technique and his mastery of an improvisational style of freehand brush drawing which was to characterize the watercolour work of so many Expressionists.

For the generation of German Expressionists that followed, watercolour proved to be a potent medium, its quicksilver quality lending itself readily to their explosive response to nature and life. Demanding a more intensive, symbolic representation of reality, a "greater depth, imagination and feeling for the human spirit", Ernst Ludwig Kirchner (1880–1938), Erich Heckel (1883–1970) and others formed the *Die Brücke* (The Bridge) group in Dresden in 1904. Experimenting with the emotional impact of colour, the high-keyed, saturated quality of watercolour suited their purpose: they used the medium energetically, combining it with crayon and gouache in a free, painterly way. Traditional techniques were abandoned, and broad areas of colour were rapidly brushed on, interspersed with black lines evoking the aggressive, jagged shapes of primitive art – an important source of inspiration for the *Die Brücke* group.

Another radical group, *Blaue Reiter* (Blue Rider), was formed in Munich in 1911 by Kandinsky (1866–1944), Franz Marc (1880–1916) August Macke (1887–1914) and Paul Klee (1879–1940), and declared that "colour is a medium of expression which speaks directly to the soul". Constructed from fragmented planes of transparent colour, Franz Marc's characteristic images of animals reveal the influence of Cubism, Delaunay and Cézanne. Marc painted animals as symbols of basic animal qualities – tenderness, vigour, strength – and also used colour for its symbolic value: blue, for example, was a 'masculine' colour, yellow a 'feminine' colour.

Similar influences are evident in the watercolours of Auugust Macke, an artist who used the watercolour

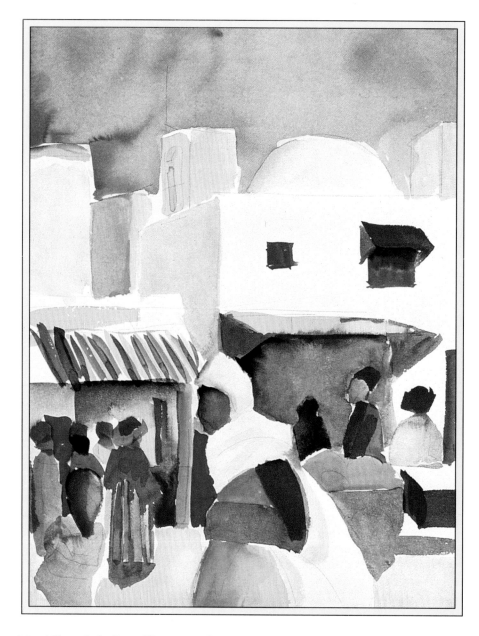

medium with skill and feeling. His watercolours painted during a trip to Tunisia with Klee shortly before his death are perhaps his most personal achievement, and are of interest for their effect on Klee, who soon after arrived at his own interpretation of the Delaunay-Macke style. Wassily Kandinsky's use of watercolour in his exploration of a spiritual dimension in art eventually resulted in abstraction, which was to occupy him for the next 30 years.

Living in Paris, the American artist Lyonel Feininger felt the effect of Cubism and, like Marc, was especially attracted to the art of Robert Delaunay. Accepting Marc's invitation to exhibit with the Blue Rider, he was closely associated with the group and contributed a delicate watercolour style employing wiry line drawing and watercolour wash, which persisted in the Precisionist works he painted on his return to America. Paul Klee (1879–1940) was another artist associated with the Blue Rider group who went on to retain a distinct identity. He too had absorbed the lessons of Cubism, especially the Orphic Cubism of Robert Delaunay. Travelling in Tunisia with Macke in

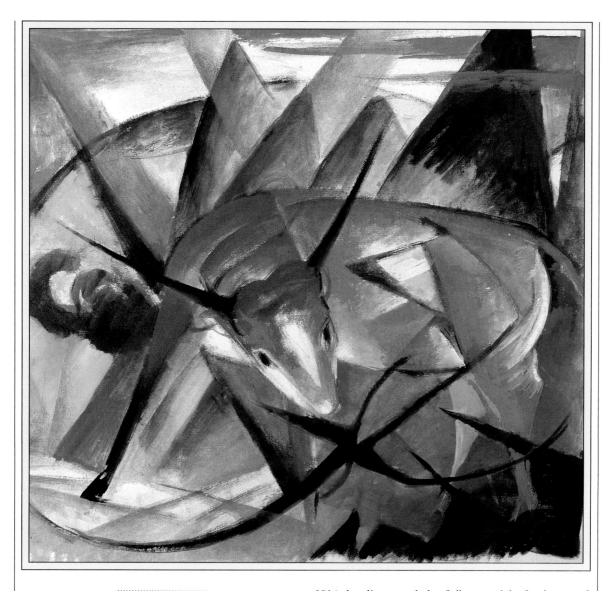

A B O V E Taureau Rouge – *Franz Marc. A founder member of the Blue Rider group, Franz Marc experimented with the expressiveness of colour and Cubist-inspired rythmic harmonies in watercolours of his favourite animal subjects.*

O P P O S I T E Tunisia – *August Macke, 1914. With echoes of his earlier work, watercolours painted in Tunisia shortly before Macke's death in World War 1 are perhaps his most personal statement. Responding to the strong sunlight and shapes of the native architecture, they consist of simply painted areas of saturated colour that recall paintings by French artist Robert Delaunay and anticipate the watercolour style of his travelling companion Paul Klee.*

1914, he discovered the full potential of colour and used grid-like patterns of flattened coloured shapes to convey the architecture and strong sunlight of North Africa. With a personal vocabulary of invented signs, childlike imagery and a softened geometry of shifting colour, Klee's watercolour work resulted in a highly distinctive and exploratory style.

An established centre for advanced thought, Vienna was also home to a forceful style of Expressionist art. The watercolours of Oskar Kokoschka (1886–1980) and Egon Schiele (1890–1918), painted during the first two decades of the century, are inseparable from the culture of *fin-de-siècle* Vienna that inspired artists like Gustav Klimt. Developments in psychoanalysis,

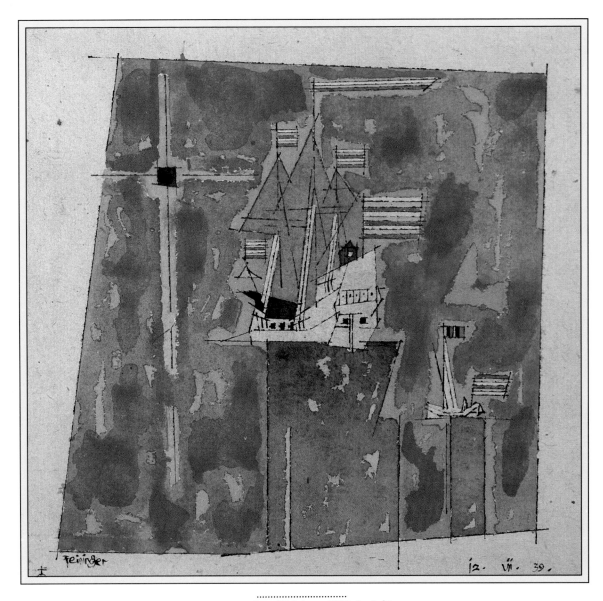

....
*ABOVE Lyonel Feininger, 1939. Invited to
exhibit with the Blue Rider group, American
artist Lyonel Feininger also taught with Klee and
Kandinsky at the Bauhaus. Boats, the sea and
shore, themes that came to dominate his work,
were especially well suited to his delicate
watercolour style.*

....
RIGHT City of Churches – *Paul Klee,
1918. One of the century's most prolific
watercolourists, Paul Klee took advantage of the
medium's transparency, building images from
areas of modulated colour occasionally
articulated by animated line drawing.*
....

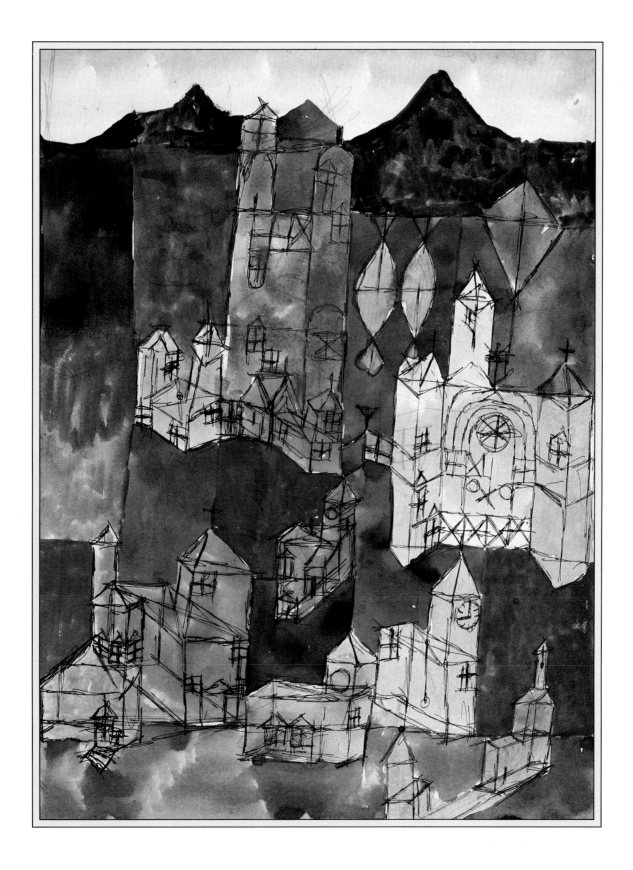

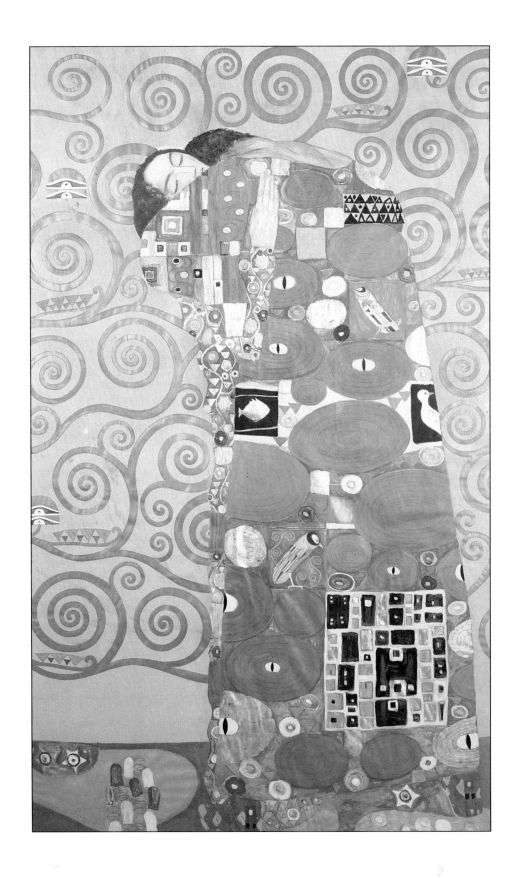

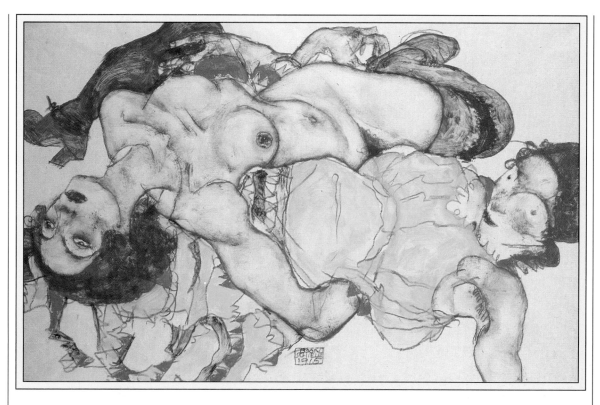

pioneered by Sigmund Freud, profoundly affected these artists, whose style of watercolour and line drawing attempted to convey the intensity of their feelings through heightened colour and expressionistic distortion of form.

Alienation and eroticism, potent elements in Schiele's work, permeated Viennese society in a period when previously hidden currents of sexuality were for the first time being brought into the open. Whereas Schiele used watercolour essentially as an adjunct to line, however, Kokoschka proceeded to experiment more fully with the medium during an extended residence in Dresden in the 1920s.

Influenced by the *Die Brücke* artists' Kokoshka adopted a bright palette and confident calligraphy, drawing with the brush in a spontaneous, freehand way that had very little to do with his earlier tinted drawings or with traditional practices. Used in such a way, watercolour's full expressive potential was explored through controlled improvisation and accident. A remarkable testimony to the boldness and luminosity possible with the medium, Kokoshka's watercolours are among the finest produced by any 20th-century artist.

The same could be said of Emil Nolde's watercolours. One of the most gifted watercolourists to emerge from the Expressionist milieu, Nolde (1867–1956) evolved a technique that, while it epitomized the free experiment championed by Expressionism, is almost Oriental in its sophistication and economy of means. Painting wet-into-wet on very absorbent Japanese paper and adeptly manipulating the medium to incorporate chance effects, Nolde worked in a bold and direct way responding equally to the changing moods of nature and to events on the paper. His paintings of flowers, stormswept landscapes and the ever-present sea reveal his desire to communicate the very essence of nature through its most intimate and elemental manifestations. Painted in the last 30 years of his life, these works represent the culmination of his achievement as a watercolourist.

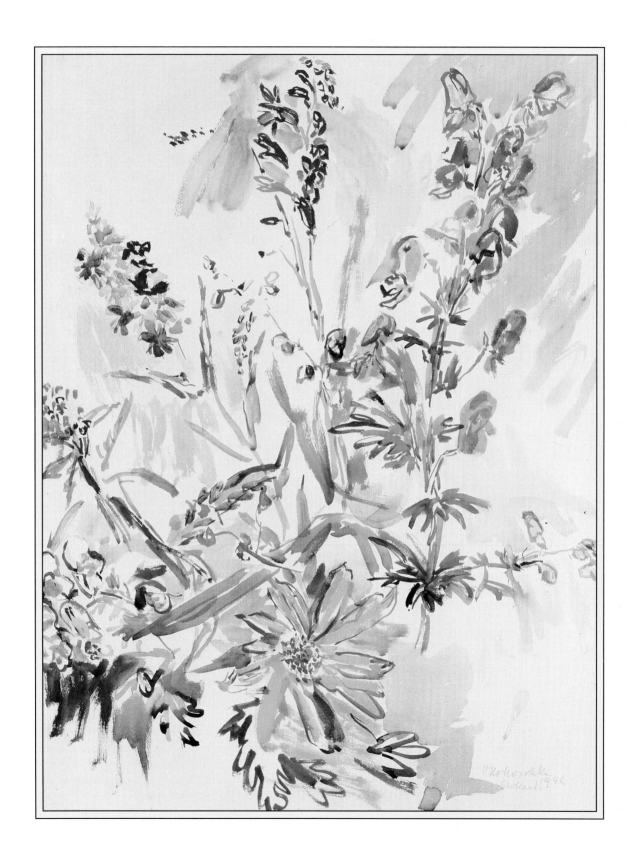

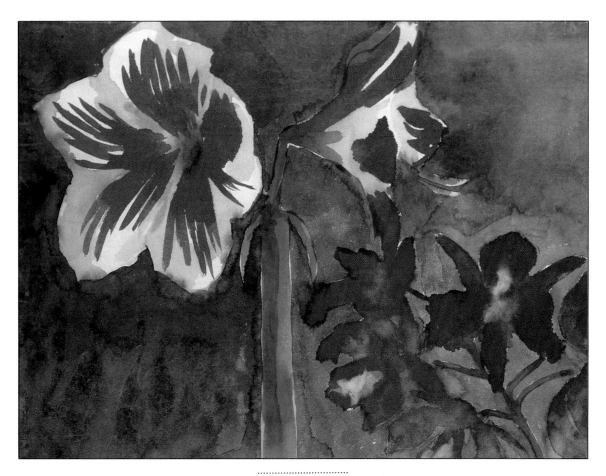

....

ABOVE Amaryllis – *Emil Nolde, c1925.*
Paintings of flowers are among Nolde's richest
works, revealing as they do his brilliant
manipulation of liquid pools of paint and
saturated colour.

....

LEFT Flowers – *Oskar Kokoshka, 1948. A*
skilled landscapist and portrait painter in the
expressionist idiom, Oskar Kokoshka's control of
the watercolour medium is clearly evident in this
striking flower study.

....

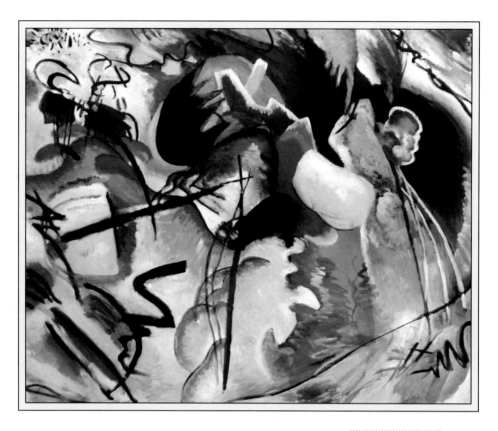

ABSTRACTION

In much 20th-century painting, the subject, or motif, has become less important than the abstract elements of colour, texture, line, shape, mass and space, and the disposition of these elements within the picture space. The importance of Cubism and Fauvism in the evolution of abstract art cannot be overestimated, but it is Wassily Kandinsky (1866–1944), a Russian artist working in Munich, who is identified most with the transition from representational to nonfigurative art. Kandinsky was a prolific watercolourist, often using the medium to initiate ideas that would be resolved in oil, or, just as frequently, employing the medium for its own sake. Searching for a spiritual dimension to art, Kandinsky recognized that each colour and form had an intrinsic expressive power that could release it from a merely descriptive role. Like other artists of the period he was intrigued by the analogy between art and music and the idea that colour harmonies could evoke musical tones. Through work that grew increasingly abstract as his career progressed, Kandinsky set about exploring such theories. It is interesting to note that Kandinsky's first truly abstract

A B O V E **Painting with White Form** – *Wassily Kandinsky, 1913. The looseness and ease with which Kandinsky used watercolour contributed to the abstract appearance of transitional works that still contained landscape elements.*

work was a watercolour (painted in 1910) and that, on returning to Russia after war broke out in 1914, it was watercolour, drawing and etching which formed the mainstay of his art.

Late in 1921 Kandinsky left Russia for Berlin and by the middle of 1922 he was living in Weimar and teaching at the Bauhaus, the art school founded in 1919 by the architect Walter Gropius. It was during this period that the number and technical range of Kandinsky's watercolours dramatically increased. Whereas previously his watercolours appeared free and improvisational, in the 1920s they became increasingly geometrical and precise. With the aid of a compass and ruler he painted flat, bright shapes which were silhouetted against pale backgrounds, the fluidity of the background washes controlled with a sponge. A layered complexity was achieved by combining positive and negative stencilled shapes and by applying watercolour spattered or sprayed with an atomizer

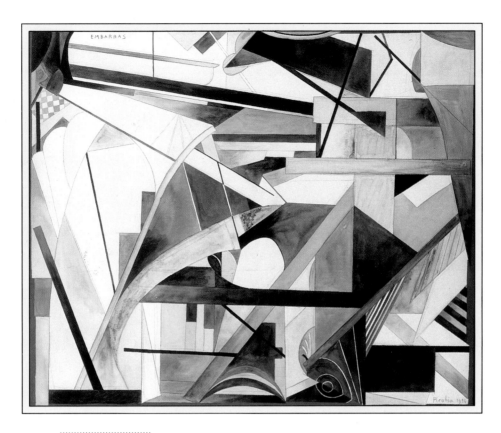

....

A B O V E Embarras – *Francis Picabia, 1914.*
Inspired by the sights and sounds of New York,
Francis Picabia made a series of abstracted
watercolours that anticipated the mechanistic
imagery of his Dada work.

....

(a technique employed by Paul Klee, who was also working at the Bauhaus). Now considered independent works in their own right, Kandinsky's watercolours far outnumbered his oils during a period that was to prove crucial to his stylistic development.

Other pioneer abstractionists working in watercolour include Francis Picabia (1879–1953) and the Czech artist Frantisek Kupka (1871–1957), both associated with the *Puteaux* group in Paris initiated by Marcel Duchamp (1887–1968) and his brothers. Like Kandinsky, they were intrigued by the parallels between abstract art and music, but while Picabia ultimately followed another route moving away from abstraction, Kupka dedicated himself to the pursuit of an abstract art, working in oil, watercolour and gouache, producing endless studies and variations on a theme entitled *Around a Point*.

In 1913, Picabia, soon to be hailed with Marcel Duchamp as the founder of New York Dada, extended his abstract *oeuvre* in a series of watercolours celebrating the sights and sounds of Manhattan. Occasionally alluding to skyscrapers or neon signs, Picabia attempted to convey his impressions of the city using abstract forms, in works which interestingly resembled contemporary works by the Vorticist artists working in Britain. As a representative of European modernism, Picabia was courted by New York's cultural élite at a time when America was being exposed to an unprecedented amount of advanced European art in The Armory Show, an ambitious exhibition of modern art touring New York, Chicago and Boston in 1913. On encountering Alfred Stieglitz, whose Photo-Secession Gallery at 291 Fifth Avenue provided a focus for new art, both American and European, Picabia quickly became part of his circle and in March to April of 1913 exhibited 16 of his New York studies at 291.

Among the American contributers to 291, a distinctive style of abstraction emerged in the work of Georgia O'Keeffe (1887–1986) and Arthur Dove; a response to European developments which was at the same time uniquely American. With an almost Oriental economy, watercolour was used to evoke the experience of the American landscape in a direct and

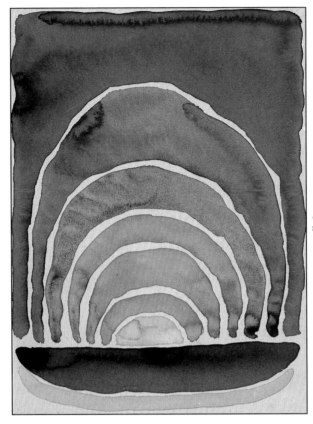

RIGHT **Light Coming On the Plains 1** – *Georgia O'Keeffe, 1917. With an almost Oriental economy, Georgia O'Keeffe used watercolour to evoke the American landscape.*

RIGHT **Blue No. 3** – *Georgia O'Keeffe, 1916. A master of controlled improvisation, O'Keeffe was able to create a striking image with just a few quick strokes of her brush.*

lucid way, the spiritual essence of nature sought through an intuitive use of colour and abstract form. Influenced by the teachings of Arthur Wesley Dow, who was currently revolutionizing art education in America, O'Keeffe combined an ability to generate abstract forms with a pantheistic vision that typifies so much experimental American art of the period. Using fluid transparent pigment and a loaded brush, she successfully captured the colours and sounds of her native land in a beautifully lyrical and sensitive way. Dove's watercolours, painted during the last decade of his life, evolved out of a lifetime's exploration of abstract forms rooted in nature. O'Keeffe's watercolour output, on the other hand, was concentrated into an intensive three-year period at the outset of her career and remained an isolated instance of uninhibited abstraction in a lifetime which brought her notoriety for the more typical hard-edged realism of her icon-like flower studies in oil.

Other American abstractionists of the period, such as Andrew Dasburg, Max Weber and Abraham Walkowitz, stayed closer to European models like Cubism, the influence of which is similarly evident in occasional watercolours by another Stieglitz artist, Marsden Hartley. The Italian Futurists were the inspiration for abstract works by the Italian-born American artist Joseph Stella (born 1935), while Stuart Davis (1894–1964) developed a personal form of Synthetic Cubism in which the flat pattern and bright colours of later Cubist paintings and collages assume a distinctly American character, recalling neon lights, jazz music and signs. Occasionally seen to contain recognizable symbols and figurative elements, Davis' work more often verges on total abstraction. The conflict felt by American artists of this period, between native realist tendencies and abstract influences from abroad, was resolved by Milton Avery. It was Avery's Fauve-inspired simplification of otherwise naturalistic subjects which led to the type of diluted modernism that flourished in America during the inter-war period, only to be overtaken by the Abstract experimentation of the next generation.

Meanwhile in Britain some remarkable pioneering works were produced under the auspices of Vorticism. The name derived from a statement of Umberto Boccioni (1882–1916), the Italian Futurist, that all

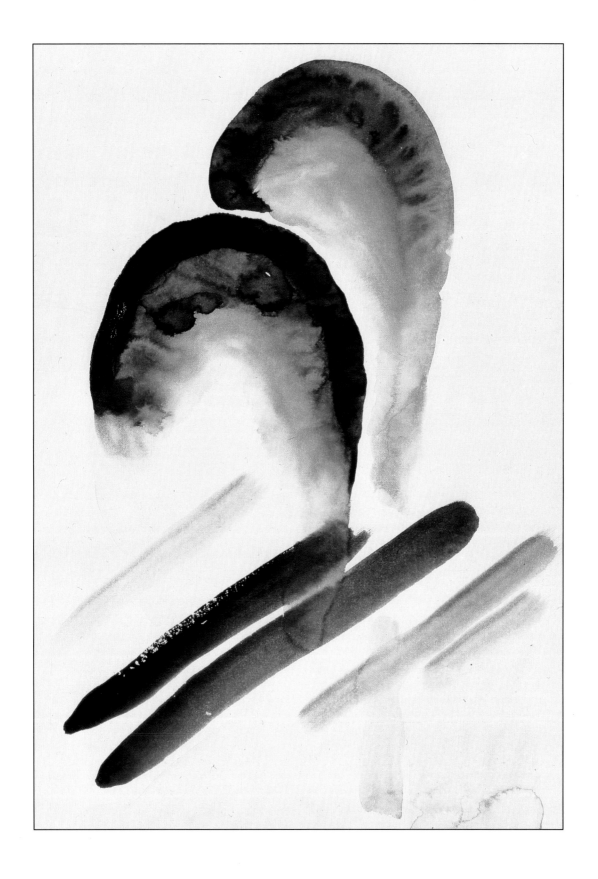

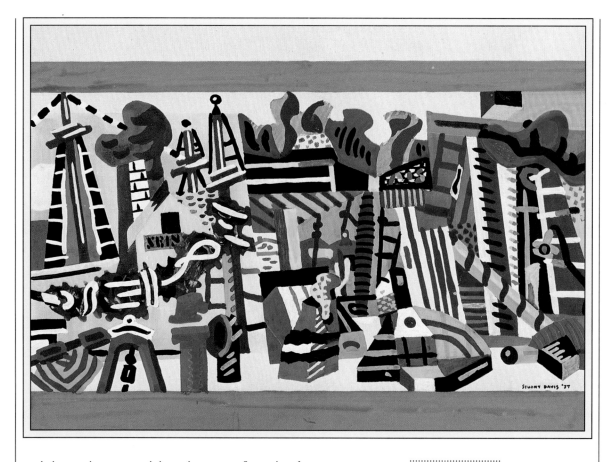

A B O V E Abstraction – *Stuart Davis 1937.*
This study for his Swing Landscape Mural
contains all the elements of Davis's distinctive
style and illustrates how watercolour is sometimes
used in a supporting role for large-scale projects.

artistic creation must originate in a state of emotional vortex. With the writer and painter Wyndham Lewis (1882–1957) at its head, Vorticism was launched in 1913 and its aims publically proclaimed in the revolutionary magazine *Blast! A Review of the Great English Vortex.* Attacking the complacency of the British art establishment, and challenging Cubism and Futurism, which he felt were insufficiently radical, Lewis advocated a type of forceful geometric abstraction. Works like *Composition* (1913), with its brittle mechanistic shapes and converging perspectives, are not only entirely abstract, an achievement which was remarkable enough at that date, but also anticipated by a year or more similarly innovative works by the Russian avant-garde. Others by Vorticist members and contributers such as William Roberts (1895–1980) and Edward Wadsworth (1889–1949), share a common vocabulary of crisply rendered geometric form. Arranged in dynamic configurations, abstract shapes were used to convey the energy and mechanical forces of modern life. As experimental works, some of which were intended for publication in the pages

of *Blast,* many Vorticist works are small-scale works on paper, painted in watercolour with chalk, pencil and collage or with ink and gouache.

Perhaps some of the most satisfying watercolours from this period in British art are those painted by David Bomberg (1890–1957), an artist associated with, but independent of, the Vorticist circle. His *Dancer* series is particularly striking for its confident handling of the medium and refined articulation of abstract form and luminous colour, as are watercolour studies preliminary to his large-scale oils of the period. Employed as a simple but evocative exploratory medium, watercolour's continued use in Bomberg's work, during and after the war, smoothed the passage from the angular style of his early abstracts to the more painterly style of his later work.

Events in Britain and America were isolated and

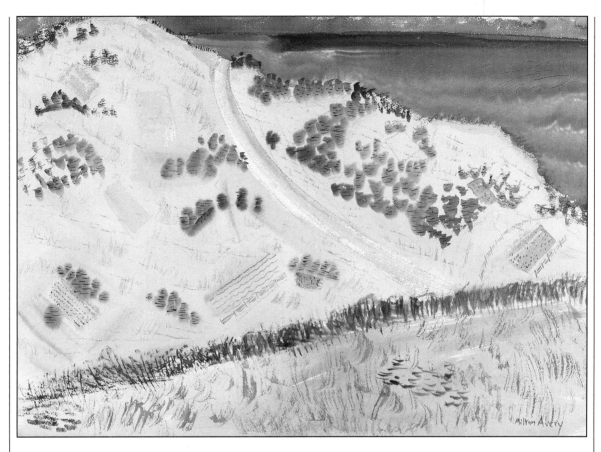

sporadic in comparison with the sustained development of abstract theory in Holland, Russia and Germany. Rigorous abstract canvases by the Russian artist Kasimir Malevich (1878–1935) confirmed his position with Mondrian in Holland as one of the principal inventors of abstract geometrical art. While Mondrian never worked in watercolour or gouache during the mature Neo-Plasticist period of his work, his colleague Theo van Doesburg – the theoretician of the *De Stijl* ('The Style') movement – did so quite often. Carrying his message abroad, van Doesburg went to Germany in 1920 and 1921 to lecture in Berlin and at the newly established Bauhaus in Weimar. Although never a member of the Bauhaus faculty, his denunciation of Expressionism was largely responsible for the greater emphasis on abstract design in the curriculum after 1923.

At the Bauhaus, and later in America, Laszlo Moholy-Nagy rallied around those seeking to unite art and technology, at the same time producing works in watercolour noted for their bold simplicity and graphic strength. Like van Doesburg, Moholy-Nagy had been deeply impressed by the work of the Russian Constructivists, who used the new language of modernism to construct radically novel forms and images rather than as an occasion for further analysis. The architectural and three-dimensional nature of Constructivist work is well illustrated in the gouaches and watercolours – sometimes combined with collage – by Alexander Rodchenko and El Lissitzky, in which geometric shapes intersect and overlap in exciting and provocative ways.

THE DADA MOVEMENT

Dada was the name given to a type of anti-rational art which erupted simultaneously in Zurich and New York during the early years of World War 1. Brought

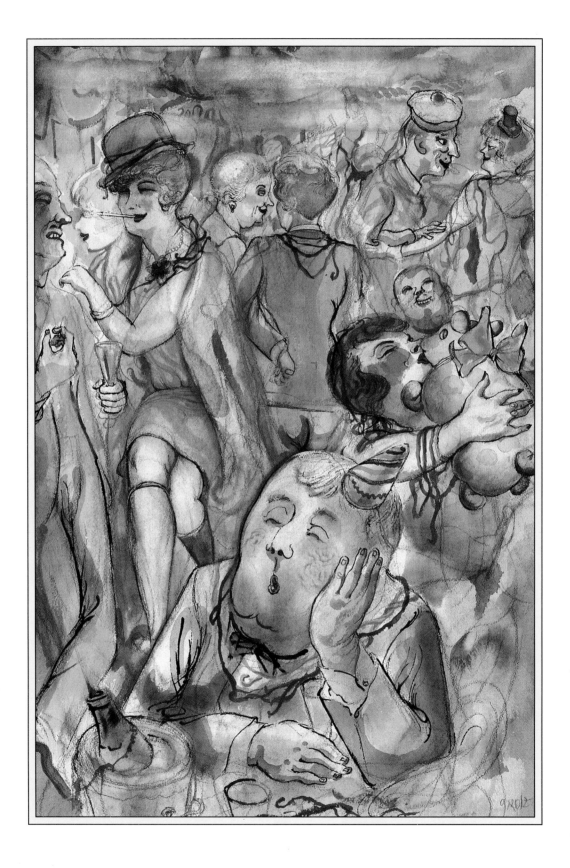

together by their horror at the futility and destruction of the war, the artists and poets associated with Dada set out to condemn the hypocrisy of the social, political and artistic climate of the times. Dada was frankly anarchistic, its attack on so-called 'civilized' society ranging from sardonic humour to savage satire. The very name Dada (from the French for 'hobby-horse') was arrived at by chance and was accepted as being suitably 'anti-reason'. In a range of work noted for its diversity, watercolour was used by the New York Dadaists for exploratory studies, combined with collage by their European counterparts in Berlin, and exploited to the full by George Grosz (1893–1959), in his satirical caricatures of postwar society.

The pioneering work of Marcel Duchamp and Francis Picabia, in Europe and New York, played a significant role in establishing the quirky and ironic style of the movement. They presented their satirical comments on society in work ranging from Duchamp's notorious 'ready-mades' sculptural pieces (substituting ordinary, machine-made articles such as a bicycle wheel or a urinal for the traditionally 'handmade' work of art), to the scatalogical humour of Picabia's witty mechanistic drawings. In studies dating from 1911–13, watercolour provided Duchamp with the means to explore analytical Cubism and photogaphic effects of motion, and to arrive at the mechanistic imagery of *Bride Stripped Bare by her Bachelors, Even*, an ambitious work on glass first conceived in 1912. Picabia, meanwhile, continued to employ watercolour throughout the erratic evolution of his own highly personal style. Man Ray (1890–1976), an American artist known chiefly as a photographer, also contributed some novel works in watercolour, using an airbrush, until then seen as the tool of commercial artists only.

After the war, ideas from Zurich spread to Berlin, which, with its established reputation for satire, quickly became the centre for a new style of Dada. To more forcefully communicate the political message of their work, the Berlin artists – George Grosz, Raoul Hausmann (1886–1971), John Heartfield and Hannah Hoch – took up photomontage, a form of collage incorporating photographic images cut out of

L E F T Study for Je Suis Un Appareil Photo *– George Grosz, c1952. One of the original contributors to the Dada movement in Berlin, Geirge Grosz forged a satirical style that persisted long after he was forced to take refuge in the United States in 1933.*

popular magazines to striking and incongruous effect. In some such works, passages in gouache or watercolour were occasionally incorporated to unify the image and supply a sense of context and space; at other times collage was dispensed with altogether and painted elements were used to reproduce the character of montage. In Hanover, Kurt Schwitters (1887–1948) devised his own personal style of collage, using found objects and scraps of paper, while Max Ernst (1891–1976), working in Cologne, used scientific illustrations and commercial advertising to evoke mysterious, dreamlike images which anticipated his contribution to Surrealism.

SURREALISM

With the gradual decline of Dada activities, the artists involved gravitated towards Paris, where their ideas were absorbed into the earliest manifestations of a new Surrealist art, officially launched in 1924. Surrealism means 'beyond and above realism', and its art is characterized by strange and disturbing images gathered from the world of dreams and the subconscious.

The only major Surrealist to use watercolour extensively was Joan Miró (1893–1983. Relying on 'automatic' inspiration, Miró capitalized on technical surprises arrived at by accident and exploited through chance. Working on paper, in pencil or ink, he combined whimsical line drawing with patches of bright colour, devising a personal language of strange animate shapes and organic forms which appear in a continued state of metamorphosis throughout his work. His pictures have a naïve beauty which recalls his admiration for the drawings of primitive peoples and of young children. With the invasion of France in 1940, Miró returned to his native Spain, where he completed a series of gouaches called Constellations. Painted as an antidote to the horrors of war, these works, with their intricate lines, coloured shapes and poetic titles, have an otherworldly quality which recalls the work of Miró's Swiss contemporary Paul Klee.

Too individual an artist to align himself with any one movement, Paul Klee refined his unique style combining free improvisation with structural principles while teaching at the Bauhaus school after World War 1. In compositions that make skilful use of watercolour's transparency, he demonstrated his absolute mastery of the medium, overlapping geometric coloured shapes to form highly evocative

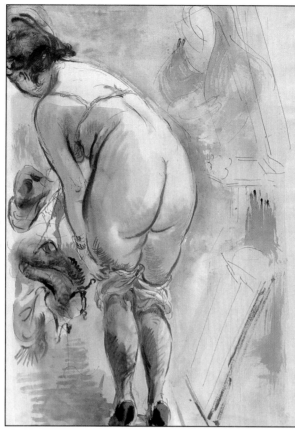

RIGHT Après La Passe –
*George Grosz, c1939. His
remorseless urge to reveal
the absurdities of life meant
that nothing avoided Grosz's
pitiless scrutiny. The flexibility
of his watercolour technique
enabled Grosz to articulate the
image and enliven the
composition by the simplest of
means.*

OPPOSITE Dimanche –
*Marc Chagall, c1937.
Juxtaposing human and
animal imagery in a world of
free floating objects and
winged figures, Chagall
created dreamlike images
alluding to his Russian past.*

abstract designs. In other examples of his work, a synthesis of signs, symbols and childlike imagery provides shrewd insights into man's position in relation to things natural and cosmic. Always humorous and ironic, his style gradually became more concentrated and prophetic and, as the years passed, thick black lines and simplified shapes replaced the delicate tracery and density of translucent colour that characterized his earlier work.

In direct contrast to the semi-abstract style of Miró and Klee, the German artists Otto Dix and George Grosz strove to confront the injustices of war through an exaggerated form of anti-idealistic realism. Whereas Dix is known chiefly as a painter in oils, Grosz must be counted as one of the major watercolourists of the century. With his commitment to satire and social comment, Grosz had thrived under the auspices of Dada, producing works combining photomontage and watercolour, caricature and mechanistic imagery. Gradually moving on from the modernist devices of his earlier work, he relied increasingly on the fluency of his watercolour tech-

nique in satirical portraits of Berlin society in the 1920s. With an ironic eye for detail he focused attention on the social hypocrisy, excesses and deprivation of Germany in the postwar years, using skilfully controlled washes and incisive line drawing. From 1933 onwards, forced to take refuge in the United States, his style became rich and sensuous as he painted wet-into-wet with characteristic ease and directness.

THE SCHOOL OF PARIS

The 1920s and 1930s were marked by continuing ferment in the art world. The presence in Paris of Diaghilev's Russian Ballet for the première of *Parade* in 1917 had proved that, even at war, Paris was still a world leader in progressive art. With Surrealism at its height and Abstraction gaining converts, Picasso decided to return to a figurative realism inspired by the classical statuary he had seen while supervising the costume and set designs for *Parade* in Rome. Massive and full-volumed, the statuesque figures of his neoclassical work are solidly modelled with

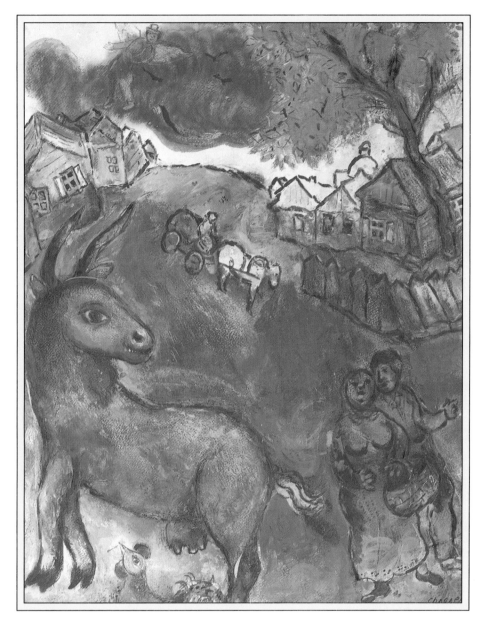

intricate hatching, so that even the smallest of them, painted in watercolour and gouache, are monumental despite their size. Newly married and with a young son, Picasso turned to the mother-and-child theme that was to recur throughout his work, and to portraits of his son Paulo dressed in the kind of Harlequin costume his father was so fond of. Another favourite theme, of figures by the sea, testifies to summers spent in fashionable resorts on the Mediterranean with his new wife Olga, a dancer with Diaghilev's ballet.

Parade marked the beginning of Picasso's involvement with the theatre. The use of watercolour and gouache for stage and costume designs, and for design work by artists in general, is a subject too vast to cover in this book; suffice it to say that Picasso produced some of his liveliest watercolour work in the form of designs for the stage. Another artist who turned to theatre design at various points in his career was Marc Chagall (1887–1985). Having studied briefly with Diaghilev's chief designer, Léon Bakst, Chagall worked first in Russia between 1919 and 1921,

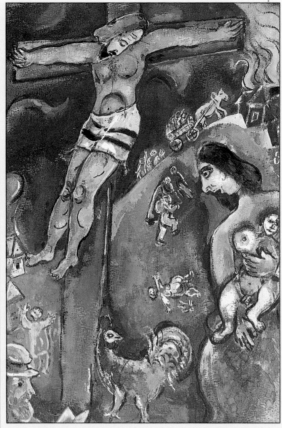

and later in the United States in the 1940s, on designs for the stage which resembled colossal enlargements of his watercolours.

By 1927 Chagall was a leading representative of the Ecole de Paris, those artists who settled in Paris during the politically unsettled period at the beginning of the century. As the 1920s drew to a close a new mood became apparent in his work, reflecting his continued preoccupation with Russia and the world of Jewish shtetls, Rabbis, peasants and peddlers remembered from his youth. In *Le Corbillard, Le Cure, et La Mort* his delight in the everyday rituals of life which, through some trick of fate, pass into folklore, is clearly apparent. With an eye for detail he captures the lively spontaneity of the scene with poetic humour, setting seemingly random patches of watercolour against flatter areas of gouache to create a well designed yet atmospheric composition.

To the Russian themes in his iconography Chagall added circus scenes, working on preliminary studies in gouache for a set of prints commissioned by his patron, Ambrose Vollard. The upside down, reversible image in *L'Acrobate*, of performer and cow precariously sharing a tightrope, is typical of Chagall's dreamlike imagery, in which the circus is seen to mirror life's absurdities. Achieving a carefully attuned balance, watercolour is used in a lively, gestural way with just enough detail added so that despite its tiny scale the painting is complete, without being overworked. Whether used alone, or in conjunction with pen and ink, crayon or gouache, watercolour was perfectly suited to Chagall's lyrical interpretation of the world, and as such appears in every phase and aspect of his work.

Among the other members of the artistic community in Paris at the time, the Bulgarian painter Jules Pascin (1885–1930) was a sensitive painter of the nude whose skilled use of watercolour washes with delicate pencil drawing proved highly popular in Paris and America in the 1920s. Pierre Bonnard (1867–1947), renowned for his domestic interiors and still lifes in oil, produced several exceptional paintings in gouache

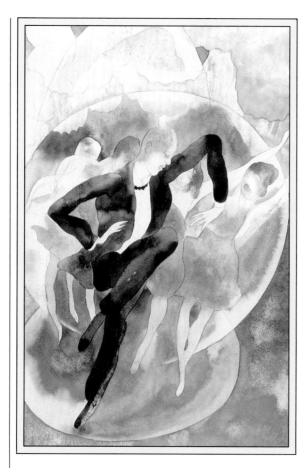

proved an important indicator that watercolour was accepted as a legitimate medium for radical experiment. A key figure among Stieglitz's American exhibitors, John Marin, must also have provided an important stimulus to younger artists: his daring and distinctive watercolours won him a prominent place among those artists seeking to Americanize the revolutionary art of Europe.

Although keen to stress the native roots of his work, John Marin (1870–1953), had clearly been influenced by Fauvism and Cubism during his years in Paris. It was only when he returned to America, first in 1909–10 and then in 1911, that Marin chose to paint the skyscrapers that were transforming the Manhattan skyline, a subject which continued to fascinate him for some years to come. Like other artists of his generation, Marin recognized that Americans could confront modernity simply by depicting their surroundings, and in particular that most powerful symbol of American modernity, the soaring architecture of city skyscrapers.

Rather than choose, as some did, to paint these modern icons in a precise and realistic way, Marin used exaggerated perspectives and viewpoints in what amounted to an almost expressionistic style, with shades of Cubist fragmentation, to capture the frenetic quality of urban life. Simultaneously, Marin was applying a modernist approach to landscape, a theme which watercolourists had been confronting for generations, and which he pursued relentlessly in a sequence of watercolours responding to the changing moods of the Maine coastline. Just as he had sought to empathize with the dynamism and vitality of city life rather than accurately record its surface details, Marin aligned himself with nature's underlying forces through a succinctness of gesture and lightness of touch perfected through his extraordinary command of the watercolour medium.

Another member of the Stieglitz group who used watercolour brilliantly and consistently throughout his short life was Charles Demuth. During the early part of his career Demuth alternated between figurative scenes of the cabaret and circus, illustration work, and a highly personal treatment of Cubist form in geometrically faceted landscapes and townscapes. The delicate combination of pencil line and watercolour wash which underpins all his work is clearly evident in the studies of fruit and flowers painted towards the end of his life, which established him as one of the masters of American still-life painting.

towards the end of his life, while Kandinsky, an experienced master in the medium, arrived in Paris after the closure of the Bauhaus in 1933. Raoul Dufy's much imitated calligraphic style was by now almost a standard component of the School of Paris, while Matisse's late paper cutouts were among the most startling works ever made using water-based paint.

WATERCOLOUR IN AMERICA

Somewhat removed from the mainstream of modernist ideas emanating from Europe, the United States continued to nurture a strong commitment to watercolour painting. Particularly suited to a type of realism represented by the work of Winslow Homer, watercolour also proved an attractive medium for the most ardent converts to European modernism and played a key role in the careers of some of America's most avant-garde artists, belonging to the Stieglitz circle.

The fact that Stieglitz chose to represent Cézanne, Rodin, Matisse and Picasso by their watercolours

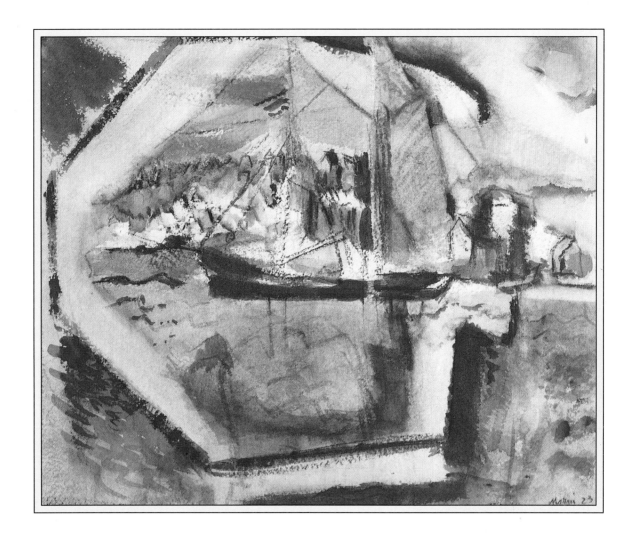

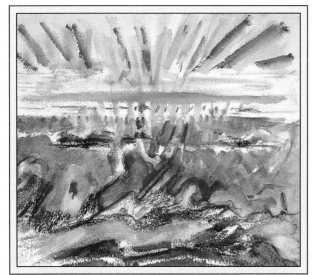

....
A B O V E Sail Boat in Harbour – *John Marin, 1923. Using Cubist devices and expressive brushwork, Marin applied a modernist approach to traditional landscape subjects.*

....
L E F T Sunset, Maine Coast – *John Marin, 1919. With an exceptional command of the watercolour medium, Marin sought to align himself with nature's underlying forces.*
....

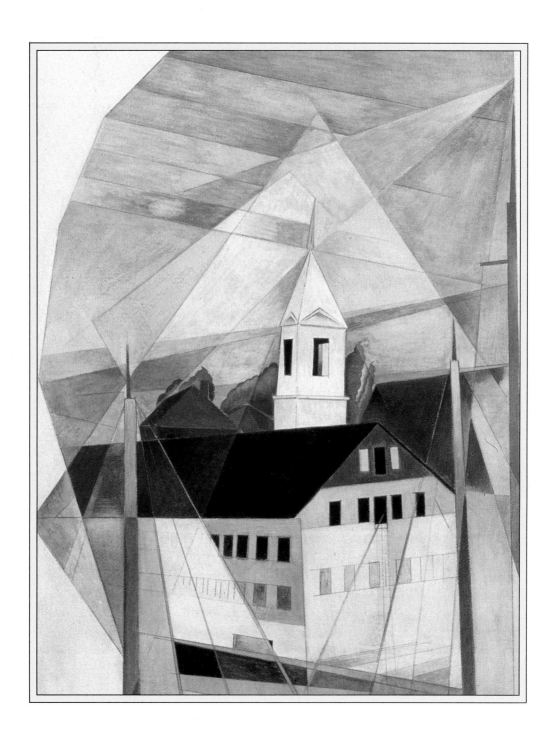

······························
A B O V E Box of Tricks – *Charles Demuth,*
1919. Demuth's most overtly modernist work, in
which structural lessons derived from Cubism
were applied to American subjects, sometimes led
to his being categorized as a Precisionist.
······························

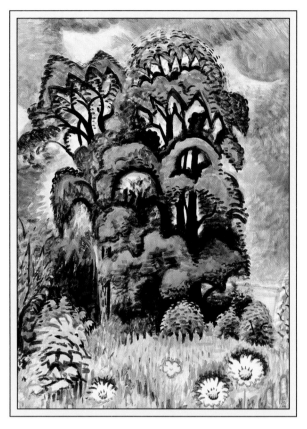

R I G H T Hush Before
The Storm – *Charles
Burchfield, 1947. With
tremendous economy of
means, Charles Burchfield
captured a very specific sense
of atmosphere with an
assurance and technical
range perfected during a
lifetime's work in the
watercolour medium.*

O P P O S I T E Adam's
House – *Edward Hopper,
1928. Heir to Winslow
Homer, the Edward Hopper's
strongly objective realism is
particularly acute in
watercolours due to being
painted on the spot.*

Demuth's most overtly modernist work, in which structural lessons derived from Cubism were applied to native land and cityscapes, sometimes led to his being categorized as a Precisionist, the name given to a group of artists whose most prominent member was Charles Sheeler. Functioning as a photographer and painter, Sheeler employed a sophisticated realist style to record the hard-edged forms and geometry of industrial American in a way which was strictly modern in its structural implications but still capable of embodying the traditional realist persuasion of American art. Although more typically an oil painter, Sheeler's study entitled *River Rouge Industrial Plant* is a fine example of his Precisionist style in the watercolour medium.

Sheeler belonged to the group of artists surrounding Walter and Louise Arensberg in New York; Charles Burchfield, confining his output almost exclusively to watercolour, preferred to work in virtual isolation in the small towns and countryside to the north of New York. The extraordinary expressionistic style of Burchfield's early work arose out of the artist's response to his immediate environment, his desire to capture the changing effects of nature and the precise atmosphere of a particular locality, rather than from any external artistic influence. With a cartoonlike simplification of form, buildings, trees and even the weather are anthropomorphized to the point of caricature to convey the intensity of his vision. Even in the 1920s and '30s, despite a shift of emphasis towards a naturalistic treatment of urban and suburban subjects, Burchfield's concern to evoke the subtle nuances of natural phenomena manifested itself in his continued use of dramatic light effects, shadows and silhouettes. His remarkable works from the 1940s, painted with an assurance and increased technical range perfected during his intervening Realist period, marked a return to the Expressionist idiom of his youth and extended over the next two decades in a series of powerful and visonary landscapes.

Burchfield's work indicates how idiosyncratic the finest American art could be in the first half of the 20th century. It also demonstrates how easy it was for American artists to move between experimentation and realism. Among those artists who provided a

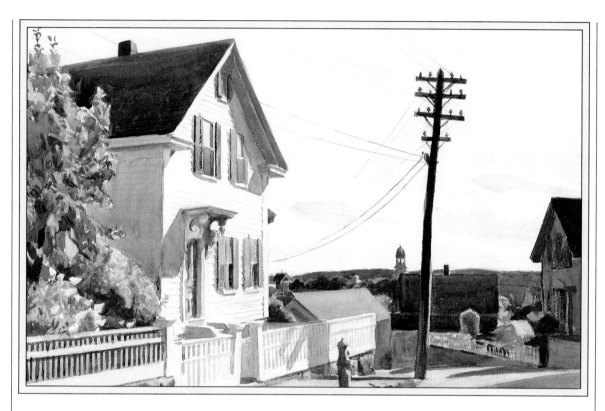

realist record of modern America, Reginald Marsh was one of the most consistent in his energetic portrayal of the minutiae of life as it was lived on the streets of New York. Like the group known as The Eight working a decade or so earlier, Marsh captured episodes from everyday life with a journalistic flair and vitality acquired through experience of the commercial art work. As an illustrator he contributed to publications such as the *New Yorker,* but unlike The Eight who – with the exception of Maurice Prendergast, Arthur B Davies (1862–1928) and George Luks – preferred to work in oil, Marsh developed a highly individualistic watercolour technique. Whereas an artist like Luks used saturated colour and dense overlays of wash, Marsh favoured a transparent and calligraphic use of watercolour combined with pen and ink line drawing, a technique well suited to his habit of incessant sketching.

Elsewhere, Regionalists like Thomas Hart Benton were mythologizing the American heartland, while politically minded Social Realists such as Ben Shahn (1898–1969) were born out of the Depression. Working in a figurative style characterized by bold, flattened forms and rich colour, Shahn's social observation was less naturalistic and more satirical than that of Marsh.

Using watercolour and gouache, he relied heavily on an inclusive line drawing of the type employed by George Grosz, who was undisputed master of a free-flowing type of satirical watercolour drawing originally formulated in Germany after World War I.

The link between illustration and the continued tradition of realist painting in America is an interesting one. It has already been noted that many of the most skilled realists had at some stage in their career worked as illustrators; Edward Hopper (1882–1967) was no exception. Forced, early in his career, to earn a living as a commercial artist, Hopper evolved a mature style which avoided the aestheticism of a more self-conscious artistic realism like that of Ben Shahn. Determined to capture a specifically American reality, Hopper painted familiar scenes of silent, sunlit streets and clapboard houses, factories, gas stations and railway sidings, with a directness most evident in his watercolours painted on-the-spot. With great economy and an utter lack of sentimentality, he depicted the cityscapes and countryside of modern America largely devoid of human presence, his objectivity tempered only by a sense of mystery and alienation that pervades so much of his work. Harshly lit, the desolate forms of his static subjects cast dramatic shadows, which inject even his most

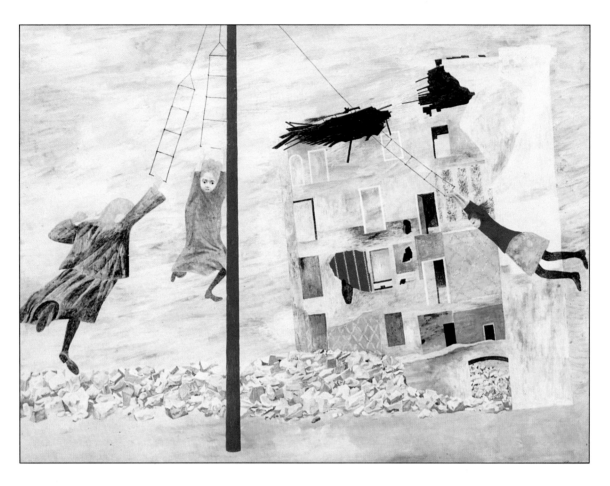

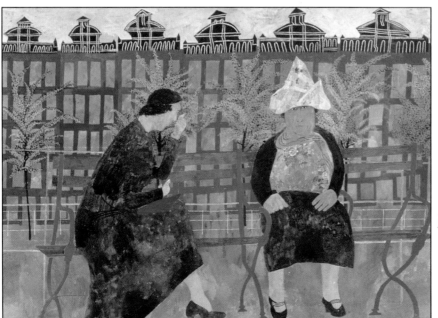

A B O V E Liberation – *Ben Shahn, 1961. With a sophisticated awareness of recent developments in art and design, Shahn treated subjects of social significance in a bold and imaginative way, relying on his sense of colour and the graphic linearity of his style.*

L E F T Everybody Reads the Bulletin – *Ben Shahn, 1946. A decorative backdrop of richly coloured repeated elements was a device much favoured by Shahn to further flatten and design his satirical figure compositions.*

insistently representational paintings with a powerful sense of structure. By juxtaposing broad flat areas of transparent wash, Hopper set down essential shapes, colours and tones, taking care not to neglect the descriptive details that give each scene its distinct identity. Employing a traditional watercolour technique borrowed from the British watercolour tradition at its purest, Hopper demonstrated his modernity by confronting 20th-century modern America in a way that was direct, uncompromising and memorable.

BRITISH WATERCOLOUR

British artists, like those in the United States, responded to Continental developments while at the same time remaining loyal to a strong indigenous tradition of watercolour painting. Two world wars brought to the fore a native tendency towards illustrative and topographical watercolour work with the need for accurate on-the-spot recording of wartime activity, while in the inter-war period, the time-honoured traditions of landscape, lyricism, fantasy and satire in British art persisted in the watercolour work of a few notable individuals, continuing to thrive in the new school of British painting called Neo-Romanticism which emerged in the closed atmosphere of the 1940s.

The years immediately preceding World War I had witnessed the rapid assimilation of Continental ideas through a series of activities including two exhibitions of Post-Impressionist art organized by the painter and critic Roger Fry (1866–1934). The formalist aesthetic of Fry and the Bloomsbury Group lay at the root of much avant-garde British art over the next few decades, while a severer form of abstraction, promoted by Wyndham Lewis (1884–1957) and the Vorticists in their journal *Blast*, was extended in the abstract experiments of artists associated with the Unit One group in the 1930s.

The outbreak of war, just a few weeks after the first issue of *Blast* was published, brought to a virtual halt avant-garde activity in Britain, and forced stylistic compromises on Lewis, whose work, commissioned through the Ministry of Information and the Canadian War Memorial Scheme, reveals an uneasy balance between the abstraction and descriptive realism of his pre-war and post-war styles. Perhaps the most oustanding of the first generation of war artists, experience of the trenches caused Paul Nash (1889–1946) to temporarily abandon his lyrical watercolours of coastal and country scenes to paint ravaged landscapes of the Western front, making him one of the most resourceful landscape artists of his generation.

With an affection for the English watercolourists, Nash evolved a contemporary interpretation of the British landscape tradition, which in turn influenced the Neo-Romanticism of artists like Graham Sutherland (1903–80). Together with his brother John, Nash virtually founded a school, and by his association with Henry Moore and Ben Nicholson, infused an element of landscape into the new abstract movement which he promoted in the 1930s through his formation of Unit One. Members Nicholson, Moore and Hepworth also belonged to the Seven and Five Society (1919–35), which included figurative artists such as David Jones (1895–1974) a poet and watercolourist in the mystical English tradition of Blake and Rossetti.

Little known outside Britain, David Jones was a watercolourist of real merit. His highly controlled yet fluid watercolours of this period, partly inspired by French examples, are typical of the lyrical still lifes and landscapes painted by members of the Seven and Five Society in the late 1920s. Responding to the work of Matisse, Jones subdued the Fauve palette, and, by using delicate watercolour washes over thin pencil lines on white paper, succeeded in capturing the pale, evocative light and atmosphere of England. By combining watercolour with bodycolour – usually white gouache – he achieved effects of brushwork and texture comparable to those attained by Ben Nicholson in oils. Persuaded by his experiences in the trenches to turn to Catholicism, Jones had worked for a time with Eric Gill (1882–1980), the stone carver, engraver and typographer joining his guild at Ditchling in Sussex and subsequently working with him in Wales and Buckinghamshire. While continuing to find inspiration in his immediate surroundings, Jones turned increasingly to historical subjects, myths and legends, acknowledging his role in a watercolour tradition that reached back through Blake to the Medieaval illuminators.

Belonging only briefly to the English Surrealist group formed in 1936, watercolourist Edward Burra (1905–76) was too idiosyncratic an artist to subscribe wholeheartedly to any artistic doctrine. Although parallels can be drawn between the inventive fantasy of some of his work and the surreal imagery of artists such as Max Ernst, Burra's sardonic eye and his specialist use of watercolour link him rather with an English tradition of illustrators, from Grandville and Cruikshank to Aubrey Beardsley. In the 1930s Burra travelled widely, visiting Spain, Mexico and New York, where he spent much of his time painting the black community of Harlem. Later he turned increasingly to still-life subjects and landscape. A visit to the United States in the 1950s inspired a further series of the type of low-life scenes for which he is so renowned. With a well practised visual memory and a sharp eye for detail, he frequented clubs and music halls, drawing also on his enthusiasm for film, jazz, popular fiction and magazine illustration. A skilled watercolourist, he devised new applications of traditional techniques to build larger and more complex images, and occasionally experimented with collage and montage. Burra tended to compose his pictures from disparate elements, remembered or borrowed, working systematically from a detailed linear drawing to a highly finished watercolour image of remarkable intensity.

WAR ARTISTS

The ravages of World War II fostered a diverse range of watercolour work, with artist-designers, including Anthony Gross, Edward Bawden (1903–1989) and Edward Ardizzone (1900–1979) making documentary records of wartime activity in the Middle East and the Western Desert. Their rapid, line and wash technique, ideally suited to the necessity of painting on location, confirmed once again watercolour's links with the tradition of illustration in Britain. Working in North Africa, then joining the allied advance on Italy, Ardizzone kept a sketchbook and diary, making written notes and rapid sketches from which he would reconstruct later pictures. Primarily interested in the human element, he captured on paper some of the less attractive aspects of victory – the looting and horrors of death and defeat – in an animated and only too memorable way.

Travelling in the Middle East, Edward Bawden sketched portraits of the native troops using watercolour, pen and ink. His large watercolour *Menelik's Palace (The Old Gebbi)* is one of the most famous and atmospheric of the wartime pictures. Eric Ravilious had, like his friend Bawden, worked in a remarkable variety of media as a mural painter, lithographer, illustrator and designer of furniture, glass and pottery, but he considered himself first and foremost a watercolourist of rural landscapes. As an official War Artist he completed some fine watercolours of British naval destroyers, submarines, coastal defence subjects and RAF seaplanes before being lost in action off the coast of Iceland. Leonard Rosoman's paintings of aircraft

carriers belonging to the British Pacific fleet were similarly permeated by a strong element of design. Working mostly in gouache but also in oil and watercolour, Rosoman completed his official war work in the Far East, recording the damage done to Hong Kong during the Japanese occupation.

War work by Graham Sutherland (1903–80), John Piper (born 1903) and Henry Moore (1898–1986) reveals the artistic preoccupations that link them to contemporary trends in British art, ranging from pre-war Surrealism to post-war Neo-Romanticism. Moore's favourite themes of the reclining figure, mother and child motifs, and the interplay between interior and exterior forms, are all present in his great series of drawings of people sheltering from bombing raids in the London Underground. His wartime experience reaffirmed the humanist side of his work, previously subordinated in his experimental drawings and abstract sculptures of the late 1930s. From the swaddled forms of the sleepers, wrapped in blankets and coats, Moore evolved his later draped figure sculptures, while his continued fascination with the merging of human forms with land forms was a central preoccupation of Neo-Romantic artists in the 1940s. His graphic technique of applying water-based paints over wax crayon, used in his wartime studies and in earlier Surreal studies of abstract form, contributed to the mixed-media technique, combining gouache with ink and chalk, which was adopted by Neo-Romantics such as Piper and Sutherland.

Commissioned, like Moore, to depict aspects of life in wartime Britain, Graham Sutherland and John Piper set about recording the scenes of devastation left by the Blitz. Perspectives of destruction in London's east end, the twisted lift shafts of city buildings, ruined churches, and the bomb-damaged Houses of Parliament, were a few of the many subjects that provided them with dramatic material for wartime records. After the bombing of London had died down, Sutherland was sent to make studies of blast furnaces in Wales, of tin mines in Cornwall, and of limestone quarrying and opencast mining – themes recalling Moore's commissioned work of coal miners in the Yorkshire pits. John Piper's earlier involvement in abstract art had been superseded by his nostalgic urge to celebrate Britain's cultural heritage, its great country houses, and its neglected churches, encountered on antiquarian rambles with poet laureate Sir John Betjeman. As an official War Artist he was commissioned to record dockyard activity in Cardiff and Southampton, violated

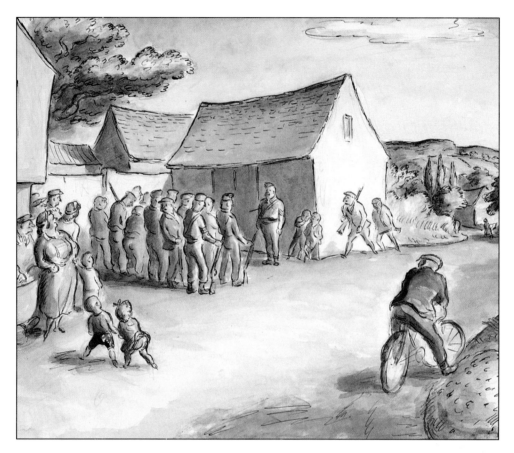

A B O V E Evening Parade of Local Defence
Volunteers (Home Guards) – *Edward
Ardizzone, 1941. At home and abroad, British
war artists found watercolour ideally suited to the
demands of making documentary records of
wartime activity.*

churches in London, Bath and Bristol, Coventry's devastated cathedral, and the Castle at Windsor, which was thought vulnerable to air attack.

Having researched his book on *British Romantic Artists* (1942) – one of a series of booklets on all aspects of British life and culture – Piper set himself the task of following in the footsteps of the great watercolourists Turner, Girtin and Palmer. His spectacular image of the limestone canyon of Gordale Scar in Yorkshire, and other innumerable watercolours of Welsh mountains and waterfalls, ruined barns and cottages, confirm how deeply he immersed himself in the British landscape and the invigoration of an indigenous Romantic tradition.

Sutherland's watercolour landscapes of Pembrokeshire, painted in the 1930s and 1940s, similarly contributed to the Romantic revival of these years. His long apprenticeship as an etcher and engraver had familiarized him with the highly charged landscape imagery of Samuel Palmer; the effects of Surrealism and the onset of war further nourished a growing disposition towards exaggerated colour and perspec-

tive, sinister mood and metamorphic stylization of form. Already, before the war, Sutherland had become fascinated by the way in which forms could be modified by emotion, partly under the influence of Picasso's studies for *Guernica*, which had impressed him when exhibited in London. Many British artists – not only Sutherland, but also Moore, Piper and a younger generation including John Minton and Keith Vaughan – recognized that by a kind of paraphrase of appearances, things could be made to look more real and vital. The fluid linearity of their frequent and experimental use of the watercolour medium enabled them to intensify the force of their message in a bold stylization of both the literary and symbolic aspects of nature which are the hallmarks of the English landscape tradition.

POSTSCRIPT

With the outbreak of World War II, the location for the most advanced developments in modern art shifted from Europe to America. New York was transformed into the art capital of the world and for the next two decades America took the lead in the new abstract and pop art movements that emerged. Since the late 1960s the expansion of the art market has resulted in a decentralization of the art world, and the growth of an international avant-garde, more diverse in its range of interests than before. The first sign of this, in the 1970s, was a renewed interest in forms of realism that had long been dismissed as archaic. More recently, there has been a re-evaluation of various forms of Abstraction and Expressionism. For the most part, watercolour has not played a significant role in avant-garde art of this period. As an exploratory medium, however, it continues to be used even by the most experimental of artists.

POST WAR AVANT GARDE

In the 1940s and 1950s, American painting underwent a revolution that very nearly destroyed the American watercolour tradition. Determined to usurp the European hegemony in the visual arts, the generation of Abstract Expressionists, or Action painters as they became known, opted for radical new methods which tended to preclude the traditional discipline of watercolour painting. Because these artists favoured large scale formats, any use of watercolour tended to be peripheral, and was concentrated in the early transitional phases of their work or used in a way that failed to exploit the innate qualities of the medium.

The most renowned of these pioneers, Jackson Pollock, employed watercolour to explore on a small scale some of the formal notions he had arrived at through his action-painting method. In a series of large scale works on paper painted towards the end of his career, Mark Rothko used water-based acrylic paint like gouache, thinning it to a gouachelike consistency or to the consistency of a watercolour wash. Mark Tobey's more frequent use of water-based media was unusual for an abstract artist of his generation. Inspired by the example of Oriental calligraphy, he evolved an 'allover' approach to composition, covering the surface of the paper with an intricate network of brush-writing in a series of works that became known as "white writing". Among the better-known Abstract Expressionists, Sam Francis was the most consistent exponent of the watercolour medium. His delicate application of brushed and dribbled translucent paint lends itself perfectly to watercolour, benefitting as it does from clean washes and the sparkle of white paper.

The European equivalent to Action painting was *l'art autre* or Tachisme – a form of abstraction in which "the mark" had an autonomous value in much the same way as "the gesture" did in American art of this period. Already before the war, the German artist Hans Hartung had painted watercolours in a calligraphic style not unlike that of his American contemporaries. Another German, Wols, specialized in small-scale drawings and watercolours, using intricate pen lines, dots and colour washes to form semi-abstract works that give the appearance of something that seems recognizable but remains elusive. A more vigorous form of expression was evident in the work of the Cobra group (based in Copenhagen, Brussels and Amsterdam) whose enthusiasm for primitive art, including child art, was shared by Jean Dubuffet. Inspired by his collection of *art brut,* Dubuffet evolved a type of art that paralleled many of the principles of Tachisme. Affecting to work in a brutal and naïve way, he manipulated materials ranging from watercolour to sand, plaster of Paris or even butterfly wings, into shapes resembling human figures or textured graffitoed surfaces.

Water-based media, especially gouache, were more frequently used by the so called 'middle generation' of abstractionists in Britain. Re-interpreting the traditionally British involvement with landscape according to current trends in abstraction, English artists like those at St Ives (in Cornwall, England), were slow to adopt the gigantic scale of American work. Some, like Peter Lanyon, combined gouache with line drawing as part of an information-gathering

....
O P P O S I T E Untitled – Mark Tobey, 1969.
Inspired by Oriental calligraphy, Tobey evolved
an allover approach to composition resembling
that of other Abstract Expressionists like Jackson
Pollock.
....

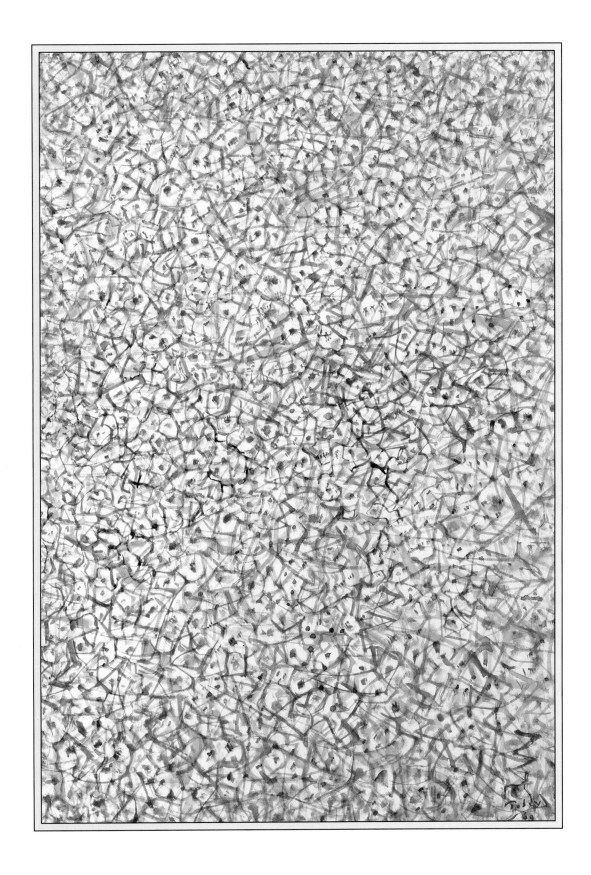

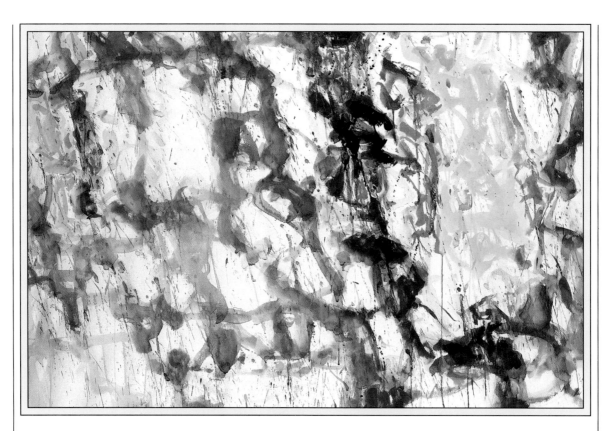

exercise indicating his journey around a particular locality. Others like Patrick Heron and Alan Davie produce whole series of independent works in gouache to exhibit alongside their work in oil.

With the exception of the New Realists and Photo-Realists, few of the artists who emerged in the next two decades employed watercolour to any great extent. An exciting range of media employed by the Pop generation rarely included watercolour while conceptual artists and earthwork specialists in the 1970s tended to use photography or video. Playing sophisticated games with illusion and reality, American artist Jasper Johns reworked motifs of target or flag in a variety of media, generally preferring more malleable materials like encaustic to watercolour while his close associate Robert Rauschenberg combined collage elements with three-dimensional objects like radios or car tyres found in the streets of New York. In later works on paper, Rauschenberg occasionally used watercolour and gouache, blending painterly Abstract Expressionist style brushwork with silkscreened images and newspaper clippings. Another Pop or proto-Pop artist, Jim Dine, repeated single motifs like the heart in much the same way as Johns had painted the American flag. Dine was unusual among the Pop generation in his willingness to pursue watercolour as an independent branch of his art. Claes Oldenburg, a leading figure in the Pop movement, used watercolour in sketches or proposals for collossal public monuments, giant scissors or a huge clothes peg, while Andy Warhol used it in drawings that reflect his experience as a graphic artist before his silkscreen image made him famous.

The increasing eclecticism of art in the 1980s has opened up new opportunities for watercolour. American artist David Salle has capitalized on watercolour's transparency by superimposing images to explore themes found in his larger paintings while European artists like Sandro Chia, Francesco Clemente and George Baselitz have also produced exciting work using watercolour. Used to a wide range of media and working, like most of his contemporaries, on a huge format, Clemente is also a skilled water-

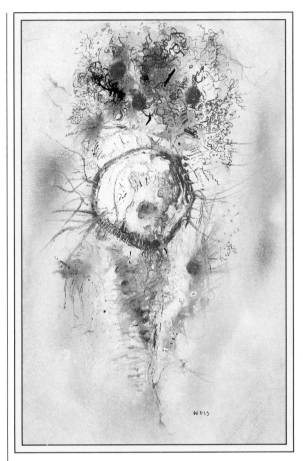

....
A B O V E Composition – Wols, c1950. *In Europe, watercolour was used by abstract artists working in a style equivalent to Action painting which was called Tachisme.*
....

colourist, producing marvellously fluid and controlled images with liquid strokes applied into wet washes. Meanwhile in Britain and America separate trends in more specialist watercolour work continue to thrive alongside these more international developments.

A CONTINUING TRADITION OF WATERCOLOUR

A recent resurgence of interest in realist watercolour suggests that traditional watercolour methods will continue to regain currency. American artist Andrew Wyeth's paintings of the people and places of rural Pennsylvania and Maine set him apart from his contemporaries in the fifties and sixties. Like Eakins and Homer, his works are traditional in technique yet modern by virtue of his fidelity to his subject. Working in washes overlaid with tiny dabs of dry pigment, a technique that Wyeth calls "dry brush", his watercolour paintings took on an increasingly detailed, highly finished appearance.

Photo-Realism, a kind of realist painting that emerged in the 1970s, and practiced by artists like Richard Estes, Robert Bechtle, Ralph Goings and John Baeder, derived from photographic imagery. Using a variety of media that frequently included watercolour, these artists sought to create the illusion of a painted photograph, in their celebration of popular culture and urban and suburban America. Idelle Weber's large-scale paintings of rubbish photographed on the streets of New York included watercolours which were among the most ambitious Photo-Realist works in the medium, while the symmetrically arranged groups of objects painted by Don Nice represent an alternative form of realism. A recent trend employing traditional watercolour technique on a large scale is exhibited in the ambitious scale of Joseph Raffael's work and a whole group of associated artists working in America today.

In Britain a strong tradition of watercolour persists in the work of artists belonging to specialist circles and societies like the Royal Society of Painters in Watercolour, better known as the Royal Watercolour Society or RWS. Founded in 1804, as an exhibiting forum for artists working in the newly-popular medium of watercolour, it represents the continued experimentation and dedication to the medium among British artists over a period extending for more than a century and a half. Internationally renowned British painters like David Hockney or Howard Hodgkin work in watercolour as well as in oil, while a particularly lively strain of watercolour work exists among Scottish artists this century. A very personal, poetic approach to watercolour was evolved by John Maxwell in the thirties and forties, which alongside that of his close associates Penelope Beaton and William Gillies teaching at the Edinburgh College of Art, inspired artists like Sir Robin Philipson and Elizabeth Blackadder working in the medium today. Elsewhere in Scotland John Bellany and a group of younger expressionists from Glasgow show a similar aptitude to the luminosity and freshness unique to watercolour.

The limitless potential and adaptability of watercolour has been proved again and again. Now, with a full-scale revival of interest in watercolour, its future promises to be as exciting and varied as its past.

PICTURE CREDITS